WOMEN IN INFORMAL SECTOR

WOMEN IN INFORMAL SECTOR

By
Dr. S. N. Tripathy
Dept. of Economics
Aska Science College
Aska
(Orissa)

2003

DISCOVERY PUBLISHING HOUSE
NEW DELHI-110002

First Published – 2003

Reprinted – 2025

ISBN: 978-81-7141-624-0

Women in Informal Sector

Published by:

DISCOVERY PUBLISHING HOUSE
4383/4B, Ansari Road, Darya Ganj
New Delhi-110 002 (India)
Phone: +91-11-23279245; 23253475; 43596065
Mobile: +91 9811179893 / +91 9871656464
E-mail: discoverybooksindia@gmail.com
orderdphbooks@gmail.com
namitwasan9@gmail.com
web: www.discoverypublishinggroup.com

Printed at:
Infinity Imaging Systems
Delhi (INDIA)

Preface

There has been continuous changes in the socio-economic lives of mankind in the wake of modernisation, urbanisation, spread of literacy, exposure to the media of mass communication etc. But ironically, females particularly in rural areas have suffered inequalities compared to their male counterparts. Both national and international agencies have began focusing their attention to the problems of women and have initiated series of programmes and activities targeted for women's development. A large number of studies have been, and are being carried out on multi-dimensional facets of women's life. These studies have helped understanding of the prevailing situations as well as assessing the effects of developmental plans and programmes on women community.

The present work which contributes to some extent towards the understanding of the socio-economic problems of informal women workers in a backward state like Orissa, is the outcome of the financial support provided by the UGC, Calcutta under minor research support scheme to University and College teachers. Drawing upon the findings of the important studies conducted on various fields of informal sector, the present research work examines the socio-economic problems of construction women labour and women employed in domestic service employment in Berhampur City of Orissa. The original report has been thoroughly reviewed in order to release it in the book form.

The study is first of its kind and although descriptive in nature in analyzing the socio-economic profile of the informal women labour, has important implications in stimulating further debate on areas of informal sector to both academics and policy makers. Here, I would like to express my gratitude to many people who have helped me at various stages of this study. To the authorities of University Grants Commission, Calcutta, I express my deep gratitude not only for their consideration of the topical importance of this study but also for providing financial support to undertake the work.

I take this opportunities to express my thanks to the Librarian, J.N.U., Central Library, New Delhi, National Library, Calcutta, N.K.C. Centre for Development Studies, Bhubaneswar for giving me the opportunities to use their libraries for the present study.

I express my thanks to my wife Meera for constant inspiration to expedite the study in due time.

Finally, for errors and omissions, I seek the indulgence of the readers.

S. N. Tripathy

Contents

Chapter—1

Introduction

An attempt has been in this chapter to portray the role of women in the economy, the multi-dimensional activities in which women do take part and more specifically, the informal sector employment. Besides, the objectives, scope, methodology and scheme of the study has also been outlined.

Women play a paramount role in the socio-economic destiny of the country: In fact, the pace of economic development of a country can be accelerated by enhancing the status, position and living condition of women in a country. Participation of women in the process of economic development is greatly acknowledged even though its degree varies from country to country. Women account for over half the food produced in the developing world, and even more in Africa, they constitute one fourth of the developing world's industrial labour force, they carry the main responsibility for childcare and household chores; they head one fourth or more of the families in many developing nations, and they usually fetch most of the household's water and fuel wood. Studies in Nepal and Philippines suggest that when the production of rural women is valued properly, on average, they actually contribute about one half of the family's income.[1]

The World Bank in its annual report in 1989 observed that 35 per cent of Indian households below the poverty line are headed by women, and in most causes, are thus, dependent exclusively on female income.[2]

Presently, women produce 50 per cent of the world's food supply, account for 60 per cent of working force and contribute up to 30 per cent of the official labour but receive only 10 per cent of the world economy and more surprisingly own less than 1 per cent of world's estate.

In Tanzania, women work an average of 2600 hours a year in agriculture, it is only 1800 hours a year for men. In Africa as a whole, 60 per cent of all agricultural work, 50 per cent of animal husbandry, and 100 per cent of food processing is done by women. For millions of women in the third world—who cook and clean, sew and wash, plant and weed, care for the old and bring up the young, a 16 hours day is not uncommon.[3]

According to the ILO more than 45 per cent of women all over the world in the age of 15 to 64 are contributing to the economy is a significant proportion. Females suffer from two sets of discrimination, firstly pre-market discrimination that is lack of access to factors such as education, training, experience and so on which develop capital and secondly to cost market discrimination namely differential wages for similar work.[4]

Conceptualizing the Informal Sector

The majority of work force today is in what is generally known as the unorganised or the informal sector, which does not require much training or education, in activities which are traditionally known as women's work such as domestic services, laundry, child minding (Ayahs) etc.[5]

According to the report of the National Commission on self-employed workers and workers in the informal sector

(a) Women doing manual work like agriculture, construction labour and other sectors.

(b) Home-based producers (including artisans and piece rate workers).

(c) Women engaged in processing work in traditional and non-traditional areas.

(d) Providers of services like washer women, scavengers and domestic help.

(*e*) Petty vendors and hawkers who do not hire labour except for taking the assistance of family members.

(*f*) And all other poor labouring women, in the unprotected sector not covered in the proceeding sections.

Report of the commission on rural; labour defines informal sector as:

1. A person who is living and working in rural area and engaged in agricultural and/non-agricultural activities requiring manual labour, getting wage of remuneration on partially or wholly, in cash or kind or both during the year.

OR

2. Such own account workers who are not usually hiring in labourers but are a part of the petty production system in rural areas.

The aforesaid two definitions, or rather, descriptions bring out the ways that production is organised in the sector.

In fact, a clear picture pertaining to the term, "informal sector" is to be outlined before focusing light on the socio-economic problems of the informal women labour in Orissa.

Though the term "Informal sector" is widely used, its precise meaning has remained somewhat elusive and the subject of controversy as it has been defined in different contexts and given in different meanings (Hussenmanns, 1997). Thus, different countries have adopted the definition which is appropriate to their needs and the system of data collection for the same. In India, the term "informal" has been used neither in the official statistics nor in the National Accounts Statistics (NAS). The terms used in the Indian (NAS) are 'organised' and 'unorganised' though quite often researcher have used the term "organised" and "informal' interchangeably. In fact, the term "informal sector' and 'unorganised' sector are quite similar to each other though not identical.[6]

In fact, Sohn Keith Host (1972) was the first to use the formal and informal sector dichotomy. Focusing as migrants in urban Ghana (Accra), he highlighted the existence of the variety of new income generating activities particularly in the trade and service categories. By virtue of the fact that most of them were in the unrecognized sector and fall outside the preview of the existing statistical data collection machinery they are labelled as informal income generating activities or the informal sector (IFS).[7]

Deepak Mazunder (1975) has brought out the distinction sharply focusing on the fact that entry into the informal sector labour market is unrestricted while that in the formal sector labour market is restricted by artificially raised hiring standards norms and procedures.

T.S. Papola (1980) has given a very simple definition. In his study on Ahemedabad, he suggests that the informal sector is convenient way of designating a segment of the economy having certain characteristics which the growth of enterprises and activities operating in this segment.

According to him, the following are the most observed features of informal sector in the studies on the subject (i) small size of operations, (ii) informal structure and family ownership, (iii) non-modern technology, (iv) lack of access to government favours, (v) competitive and protested product market, (vi) unprotected labour market.

Todaro analyses the features of informal sector as: "The informal sector is characterised by a large number of small-scale production and service activities that are individual or family owned and use labour-intensive and simple technology. The workers in this sector have little education, and generally unskilled and lack capital resources. As a result, worker's productivity and income tend to be lower in the informal sector than in the formal sector. Worker's in this sector do not enjoy the measures of protection offered by the formal sector in terms of job security, decent working conditions and old age persons. Most workers entering this sector are recent migrants from rural areas unable to find employment in the formal sector. Their motivations is usually to obtain sufficient income for survival purposes rather than necessarily for profit, relying on their own indigenous resources to create work."[8]

It is inferred from the above-started analysis that in developing countries the rural poor failing to get absorbed in the agricultural sector and formal sector, are forced to migrate to urban centre with a view to searching employment, income and livelihood. They are mostly engaged in the retail trade like selling vegetables, pan, repairing shops, tea stalls, and as casual labour in construction, shops and commercial establishments, hotels or restaurants and domestic households. All these are known as 'informal sector'.

URBAN LABOUR FORCE IN URBAN INFORMAL SECTOR

Recent studies reveal that the share of the urban labour force engaged in informal sector activities ranges anywhere between 20 to 30 per cent.

Table—1
Estimated size of urban labour force in the informal sector in selected developing countries

Area	*Share*
Africa	
Abidjan, Ivory Coat	31
Logost Neseria	50
Kumasi, Ghana	60-70
Nairobi, Kenya	44
Senigal	50
Tunisia	34
Asia	
Calcutta, India	40-50
Ahmedabad, India	47
Jakarta, Indonesia	45
Colombo, Srilanka	19
Thailand	26
Pakistan	69
Latin America	
Peru	60
Venejuala	44

Source: Sethuraman, S.V. "The Urban Informal, sector in the Developing Countries," (Geneva, ILO, 1981).

Dr. Samal, in his study of Urban Informal Sector (1990) States, "Inadequate income and poverty in the native place", mentioned by about 44.14 per cent of migrants and constituting about one-third of the total frequencies of multiple response was found to be the single most important cause for migration out of seven different factors suggested in the questionnaire. The finding is also similar to the implicitly or explicitly stated by several other scholars (Azis; 1984, Dandekar and Rath: 1971, Mydral, 1968, Oberal; 1983, Papola: 1981, Santos: 1979)[9]. In fact, there is no denying of the fact that poverty alone compels people to abandon their native land.

Table—2
Frequency Distribution of Migrants in Sample Workers by Motive/Cause

Sl. No.	Motive/Cause	Response	Each alternative as and total response	Each alternative and to total migrants
A	Inadequate income and poverty in native place	49	33.33	44.14
B	Unemployment/Under employment in the native place	5	3.41	4.51
C.	Loss of property and source of income due to natural calamities	7	4.76	6.31
D.	Opportunities for year-round employment in Sambalpur against seasonal employment in rural area	6	4.08	5.41
E	For more expected life-time income in Sambalpur in comparison to the native place	30	26.53	35.14
F.	Following the primary migrant	25	17.01	22.52
G.	Other (quarrel with family members etc.)	16	10.88	14.41
	Total	**147**	**100.00**	

Source: Samal, K.C. "Urban Informal Sector" Manak Publication, Pvt. Ltd., New Delhi, 1990, p. 68.

Reasons for the Growth of Informal Sector

The growth of employment in the organised sector in India has been falling steadily between 1973 and 1994 (Table—3). This is true for almost all industry groups, which implies that the growing labour force can not be fully absorbed within the shrinking organised sector. Given that open unemployment rates in India have not increased over the period, the labour force was absorbed in agriculture and in the unorganised informal segments of the non-agricultural sectors. In effect, this led to an increase in women's employment in the informal sector.

The growth of ancillarisation and industrial employment through sub-contracting combined with a steady fall in incomes of households due to the poor performance of the economy as a whole and additional factors that account for this increase in the number of women entering the informal sector. The reasons for the growth of the informal sector are important from the point of view of formulating policies. The process of globalisation, export-oriented industrialisation and relocation of industries from the developed to the developing countries also contributed for the growth of informal sector.[10]

With the growth of industrialisation and urbanisation, landless labourers in the absence of assured source of employment in rural areas, migrate to urban areas in search of employment. In urban areas, women are generally employed in formal sectors like weaving, handicraft, tailoring, sale of fish and construction activities.

Moreover, the alarming rate of growth of population in developing countries has represented in an increase in the rate of labour supply in cities and towns. This huge migration of rural poor to the urban areas in search of work and livelihood reflects the spill-over of rural poverty. Along with this process, it has been recognised that there is a dichotomy in urban economies in developing countries. Whatever, may be the reasons, economic development failed to generate adequate employment and income opportunities particularly in the modern formal sector. Under the circumstances, the surplus labour force has been compelled to find its own source of employment and hence, of survival. Thus, the growth of informal sector employment emerged with its multi-dimensional coverage.

Table—3
Growth in Organised Sector Employment (1974-94)

Sector	*1973-78*	*1978-83*	*1983-88*	*1988-1994*
Agriculture	2.22	1.30	1.11	0.35
Mining and quarrying	5.20	2.56	0.88	1.04
Manufacturing	2.30	2.08	–0.09	0.04
Electricity, Gas and Water Supply	3.27	3.67	3.26	1.58
Construction	–1.95	1.91	1.25	–0.62
Trade	–13.26	1.94	1.43	1.56
Transport, Storage etc.	1.62	2.25	1.20	0.42
Services	4.31	2.96	2.25	1.76
Total organised	2.45	2.48	1.38	1.00
Public Sector	—	2.99	2.17	1.00
Private Sector	—	1.41	–0.43	1.18

Source: Successive Annual and Quarterly Employment Review, Ministry of Labour, New Delhi, Quoted in Shariff and Gumber (1999).

Review of Literature

Rural women's contribution in development of rural sector and in the national economy has been one of the most neglected, under-estimated, over-looked and discriminators assessed area of studies. Moreover, studies on women in the informal sector is extremely limited.

A study conducted by the ILO established that worldwide, only 27 out of every 100 women were found to be economically active. Further, the participation of women in economic activities is controlled by the social and cultural conditions prevailing in particular regions.

In Eastern Europe and the USSR 40 per cent of women are part of the work force where as in Latin America less than 15% of women work outside the home. In some developing countries such as India, Malaysia, Morocco and Tunisia etc. women's participation varies between 30 to 40 per cent of the total "agricultural" work force, this constitutes 20 to 25 per cent of the total "agricultural" work force, this constitutes 20 to 25 per cent of the total female population.

Further, it has been observed that discrimination against women in terms of employment opportunities, wages, working conditions, promotion avenues is a common phenomenon all over the world.

In India, some of the vital aspects of informal sector are totally neglected in research. Moreover, most studies in India have been carried out in metropolitan cities such as Bombay, Ahmedabad, Calcutta, Delhi, Bangalore.

A study conducted by Thippaiah (1989)[12] examined the problem of Urban Informal sector in the Bangalore metropolitan area with the help of interview method to collect field data which has inter alia, the following inferences.

Women workers in urban unorganised sector can be broadly grouped into the self employed and the wage employed. Among the self employed there are those engaged in papad making, masala making, embroidery work, zari work, envelope making, beedi rolling, agarbathi making, match splints making, retail trading, waste paper collection and so on. The wage employed are mostly skilled, semi-skilled, unskilled and casual workers. They also belong to the category of contract workers in construction activities, industrial and commercial enterprises. In addition, women workers are also manifested as paid on piece rate basis or part-time, full time domestic servants for a fixed payment.

In self-employment activities who earn their livelihood independently or with the co-operation of family labour constitute an overwhelming majority.

A vast segment of women in the urban informal sector are migrant families to the city of Bangalore at different points of time on account of draught, jobs and marriages and wage differentials between urban and rural sector. Most of them are in the age group of 18 to 32 years, and live in slums, small towns which are devoid of basic amenities. The informal women labourers are paid low wages and their wages are just around the subsistence level, proper medical facilities and safety measures are not guaranteed for these women who work in hazardous materials such as chemicals in dyeing or cement dust in construction work.

Dr. Samal (1990)[13] has studied the economics of informal sector of Sambalpur town with the help of questionnaire and interview method. The questionnaire sought information about the enterprise, the workers engaged as self-employed or wage workers in these enterprises. The manufacturing, trade, transport, service etc., enterprises have been surveyed.

The significant findings of the study inter alia, are as follows:

Though few entrepreneurs earn a comfortable income, about two-thirds of the informal sector participants families are poor since their per captia income is less than the "Poverty line".[14]

The earnings of about one-fifth of entrepreneurs, own-account workers and wage labourers is below the minimum wage fixed by the Government of Orissa.

The informal sector units have backward linkages through input, credit and partly through acquisition of skill and technology. About 31 per cent of total sample units have direct backward linkages fully or partly with the formal sector for their inputs/raw materials/commodity used or traded.[15]

Chances of greater exploitation are higher in the unregulated and unorganised segment like the informal sector.

Tripathy and Das (1991)[16] have examined the problem of informal women labour in the tribal district of Orissa. The study based on primary data collected through a field survey conducted at the Micro level covering Phulbani town analyses the growth and size of informal labourers in the study area. The sample consists of 25 construction labourers, 25 maid servants, 25 washer women, 25 sales women and vegetable vendors and

25 from allied groups. Thus, a total of 125 households covered with a view to assessing economic conditions and work character of informal labourers.

The study brought to light that tribal women of Phulbani though cannot enter formal sector jobs because of low education and training, they contribute a significant amount to total family income through their engagements in IFS activities.

The study points out they were less than 50 per cent of women labour force are in the age range of 15-60 years, 33 per cent of the sample labourers one below the age of 15 years. Hardly 8 per cent of women labourers have school education up to 8-9 years. Women engaged in washing activities belong to 98 per cent who are mainly belonging to Khand, Gouda, Panda, Suda, Keute Castes.[17]

An important factor determining the amount of income of the informal households, is the size of landholdings from the study it was revealed that 38.4 per cent of the workers have no land, 32 per cent have a marginal land, 23.2 per cent a small size of land holding and 6.4 per cent have landed property of 5 acres and above. The study further pointed out that the maid servant's income is the lowest among all categories of informal workers. Most of women belonging to this category are divorcees, widows and younger girls.

Tripathy (1996)[18] in his paper, "women labour in construction sector" analysed the socio-economic conditions of women construction labour in Ganjam district (Orissa) with the help of data collected through sample interview and questionnaire method.

The study observed that ignorance, tradition-bound attitudes, lack of skill, seasonal nature of employment, heavy physical work, lack of job security, long hours of work, lack of minimum facilities, at the work place, ill-treatment and bondage are some of the features of the employment of women in construction sector.[19]

The foregoing analysis clearly demonstrates that research studies on the problems of informal sector, specially in smaller cities are extremely limited. Moreover, no study on informal women labour in the construction and service sector has been conducted so far.

In view of the afore-said considerations, the present study on the socio-economic problems of informal sector in Berhampur town of Orissa is first of its kind, and therefore, seems more justifiable. Obviously, this study makes an attempt to fill the research gap and focus light on the various dimensions of socio-economic problems of women labour. Thus, the findings of the study can be generalized in the context of Orissan economy and appropriate policy paradigms can be formulated in order to ameliorate the conditions of women labourers.

Objective of the Study

The present study has the following important objectives:

(i) To estimate the rate of participation of women labour in various sectors, the cause and consequences of such informal women labour in the rural as well as urban economies of Orissa;

(ii) To study the socio-economic profile of the Ganjam district and the study area;

(iii) To examine the socio-economic problems of women labour employed in the construction and service sector of the economy;

(iv) To suggest policy implication of the study for ameliorating the living condition of informal women labour.

Methodology

Keeping in view the constrains of time and cost, it was decided to collect data from Berhampur Municipality (Ganjam District). Thus, the study has been based on primary data collected through field surveys at the macro-level covering 10 different wards, selected on random sampling technique. From each ward, 5 construction women workers and 5 domestic maid servants and thus, a total of 50 construction women workers and 50 domestic maid servants have been selected at random.

The schedules and questionnaire contained items like bio-data of the respondent age, education, marital status, size of the family income, asset position, indebtedness, wage payments, working hours, nature of job, behaviour of the employer, social awareness etc.

First of all, after selecting the list of respondents, contracting them in their work place the houses were identified to conduct interview confidentially exclusively for the purpose of research study. The respondent women construction labourers originated from various villages like Lochapada, Bhabinipur, Khodasing, Lanjipalli, Narendrapur, Dakhinpur and maid servants were from various localities and slum areas. Therefore, the data were collected through questionnaire, interviews, observations and field notes by visiting several rounds to the work-sites and their native villages during their leisure (during the period May 2000 to October 2000).

In addition to the primary data, secondary sources of data have also been collected from various reports, books, Journals for the present study.

Collected field data have been arranged in the tabular from, followed by their analysis and interpretation.

Scheme of the Study

The study has been presented in the following five chapters.

Chapter—I

Introduction

This chapter deals with significance and sector, review of literature, objectives of the study, methodology and scheme of the study.

Chapter—II

Informal sector employment to women labourers:

This chapter portrays the role of women in the informal sector.

Chapter—III

A profile of the study area

The socio-economic and demographic profile of the Berhampur city have been focused in this chapter.

Chapter—IV

Socio-economic features of informal women labourers:

Socio-economic features of informal women labour have been analysed in this chapter based on field data.

Chapter—V

Concluding observations and policy implications of the study:

This chapter presents the summary conclusions and policy implications of the study.

Bibliography

REFERENCES

1. Dr. I. Satya Sundaram., *'Plight of Unorganised Women Workers'* (1996), in S.N. Tripathy (edited) Unorganised Women Labour in India, New Delhi, Discovery Publishing House, p. 2.
2. *Ibid.*
3. *Ibid*, p. 4.
4. Arunachalam, Jaya (Dr.)., *Women in the Informal Sector: Need for Policy Options* (1997), Social Welfare August-September, p. 37.
5. Jhabula Renna., *Women in People's Sector: Experiences of SEWA (1997)*, Social Welfare, August-September, p. 49.
6. Kulshrestha, A.C. and Singh, Gulab., *'Gross Domestic Product and Employment in the Informal Sector of the Indian Economy'* (1999).

   The Indian Journal of Labour Economics, Vol. 42, Number-2, p. 217.
7. Tripathy, S.N. (Dr.) Das, Soudamini., *'Informal Sector Labour in India'* (1991), New Delhi, Discovery Publishing p. 4.
8. Todaro, M.P., *"Economic Development in the Third World"*, Orient Longman Ltd. p. 283.
9. Samal K.C. (Dr.)., *Urban Informal Sector* (1990) New Delhi, Manak Publications Pvt. Ltd. p. 68.

10. Unni, Jeemol and Rani, Uma *'Informal Sector: Women in the Emerging Labour Economics,* vol. 42, No. 4, pp. 625-626.
11. Yadav, Ravi, Prakash., *Women Workers Worldwide* (1999), Social Welfare, August, p. 4
12. P. Thippaiah., *Women Workers in the Urban Unorganised Sector* (1989), Social Welfare, May p-21-22.
13. Samal, K.C. (Dr.) Op. cit.
14. *Ibid,* p. 94.
15. *Ibid,* p. 110.
16. Tripathy, S.N. (Dr.) Das Soudamini Op. cit.
17. *Ibid* p. 73.
18. Tripathy, S.N. (Dr.)., *Women Labour in Construction Sector: A Study in Orissa* (1996) in S.N. Tripathy (edited), 'Unorganised Women Labour in India, New Delhi, Discovery Publishing House.
19. *Ibid* p. 120.

Chapter—2

Informal Sector Employment to Women Labourers

This chapter focuses the theoretical background of labour market, wage differentials and their relevance to women labour in the informal sector. Besides the role of informal sector and the plight of women labour has been discussed in this chapter. In the pre-independence period, it was observed by the Royal Commission on labour that lack of mobility, wage discrimination, ignorance of the market condition on the part of the labour are the common features of the Indian Labour market. The loss of land through indebtedness, quarrel, death of the title holders and other causes, bring fresh recruities to the industrial population in India. The means of transport and communication have offered a way to escape from starvation in times of drought and floods by creating employment in industrial centres. Moreover, culture, tradition and social feelings combine to influence and generate an unfavourable occupational discrimination among women labourers vis-a-vis male labourers.

After independence, though the situation improved because of provisions granted for industrial labourers, but women informal labourers are in the grip of wage differentials due to the traditional attitude towards them by the employers. Needless to mention that in most cases, low paid informal women labourers are driven by the death or illness or unemployment of male earning members. Moreover, the poverty of the households and inability of the male members to generate adequate income are the factors compelling women workers to seek employment recruiting in low supply price of labour.

Explanation of Labour Market theories Relating to Unfavourable wage for Women

The changing labour force participation rates of women and persistently lower wage payments are the issues of deep caution for the economists in recent decades. There are views presented by economists which can be pointed out as orthodox labour market analysis, human capital theory, the economics of discrimination and segmented labour market theories.

The Orthodox Labour Market Analysis

This theory assumes that wages and employment are determined by demand and supply. Again, demand is determined by the marginal productivity of homogenous units of labour. There will be one wage rate at which the supply and demand for labour will be in equilibrium. It assumes that the employers of labour make no discrimination between labourers other than on the basis of their marginal productivities. As a result, the bulk of literature on labour markets until recently was of men's occupations and the relative wage levels between them unless it was stated as women specifically.

An analysis of these orthodox labour market theories suggest that jobs are differentiated by the income they command, which in turn, is determined by the quality of labour and consequently, incomes are differentiated. Existence of wage differentials may be because of labour market imperfection. Beeker[1] and Arrow[2] assume that discrimination exists in labour market but still under competitive condition, employers who discriminate make comparatively labour profits than the employers who do not.

Human Capital Theory

This theory assumes demand for labour to remain stable and therefore, differences in labour productivity on the supply side will be the main source of difference in earnings. According to the human capital theory, an individual can make on investment in himself or herself by devoting time for education, acquiring skills and work experience. The statement of this theory is that it would bring a higher return to an individual for making a larger investment and vice versa.

Mincer[3] and Polachek[4] remark that women in general have different expectations from men and therefore women make different investment decisions. Since women are all assumed to plan to abstain themselves from work for child bearing, they are expected to choose the low depreciation, occupations and hence in most cases they accumulate inadequate human capital and have lower life-time earnings as a result.

As a matter of fact, the occupations preferred of selected by women informal labour are defined as less productive and less skilled and therefore, become less rewarded occupations. Moreover, since the human capital concept depends heavily on the assumption that labour is paid equivalent to its marginal product and as such, the problem of measuring productivity appears as in the case of orthodox theory. Again, measurement of worker's productivity taking years of schooling alone into consideration while ignoring the important quality differences tells upon the real value of labourers and as a result, payment of wages on the criterion of number of years of schooling or training would provide a misleading conclusion. Therefore, differences in earnings need to be attributed to factors other than education and training.

Stighitz[5] and Madden[6] have remarked that imperfections in labour markets are responsible for wage differentials and thus, discrimination leading to involvement of trade union, minimum wage legislation, monopoly power etc.

Secondly, over-crowdedness in women specific jobs cancels excess support of informal labour and ultimately, results in diminishing marginal productivity.

Thirdly, in certain cases, the radial discrimination perpetuated the segmentation of the labour market in to primary and secondary sectors. The blacks were restricted to do some occupations because of the race to which they belong.

Fourthly, the internal labour market concerns itself with the rules made within the firm of craft to fixed wages and allocate labour among alternative users. The internal labour market is controlled more by institutional rules which are not always compatible with the assumptions of the competitive labour market. The internal rules govern the relationship between labourers and employers, the employer does not necessarily act as the competitive model assumes. Reduced mobility is one of the main ways in which institutional rules isolate labourers in the internal labour market from external competition.

In our country, so far as agricultural sector is concerned, as per 1991 census, the male cultivators have increased by 11.67 per cent from 7.67 crore in 1981 to 8.56 crore in 1991. The female cultivators, however increased at much faster rate of 45.23 per cent, from 1.48 crore in 1981 to 2.16 crore in 1991. The number of male agricultural labourers increased 31.48 per cent but that of female by 36.15 per cent. Seventy four per cent of the entire female working force are engaged in agricultural operations which is the largest informal sector.

Women labour is primarily involved in specific operations on the farm such as transplanting, weeding and harvesting while male labour, in general, is involved in sowing, spreading fertilizer, threshing and so on.

Notwithstanding all this discrimination and unfair deal, women play a vital role in agricultural development. Similarly, in other sectors like construction sector and service sector informal women labour play a significant role in contributing to the economic wellbeing of such households from which they originate.

Informal sector plays a vital role in a developing country like India with its abundant supply of labour. In spite of our continued effort to accelerate the tempo of economic development through Industrial enterprises only a major percentage of population are employed in the organised sector. With in agriculture, industry and services a large segment of 90 per cent of work force earn their livelihood. Fuelled by high rates of population growth, limited employment opportunity in the agricultural sector, lack of sectorial diversification within the rural economy, the cities and towns are looked upon as centres of labour absorption. They often, promote a dualistic pattern of economy. They on the one hand attract large scale, organised and formal economic activities at a limited level and on the other hand induce growth of unorganised and informal production units that absorb none of the growing labour power[7].

Women and Informal Sector

Although women are under enumerated in the official statistical system because of their casual nature of job, they play a crucial role. Thus, the actual economic participation of women in developing countries is much higher than reported through the official statistical system. While the macro-level secondary data reveal low female participation rates, micro-level studies exhibited that women, particularly in low income households participate in the workforce to a greater extent.

Moreover, in these countries a higher per centage of Urban women labourers are employed in the informal sector who are invisible, scattered, and under-enumerated.

Table—4
Work Participation Rates in Urban India

Source	*Year*	*Work Participation Rate %*	
		Male	*Female*
Census of India (Main+marginal workers)	1991	49.38	9.17
NSS 43rd Round (Principal+Subsidiary workers)	1987-88	50.60	15.20
NIUS Survey (Main+marginal workers in on income households)	1988	49.29	30.94

Source: The census work participation rates are estimated excluding Jammu and Kashmir

It is demonstrated from the Table—4 that the Urban women participation rate was 9.74 per cent for main and marginal workers put together as per 1991 census. The NSS recorded a relatively higher urban female participation rates o! 15.20 per cent for principal and subsidiary workers in 1987-88.

The NIUA survey conducted in Bangalore, Lucknow, Visakhapatnam, Faridabad, Trichur, Puri shows that for all ages women participation rate in low, income households is a high as 30.94 per cent. If women in the working age group of 15 years and above are taken into account, the women participation rate is about 50 per cent. The female work force participation shows an increasing trend as revealed from the Table—5.

Table—5
Women Workforce Participation Rates by Rural/Urban

Particular	*Rural areas*			*(In percentage Urban areas)*		
	1973	*1983*	*1991*	*1973*	*1983*	*1991*
Women workforce Participation Rates	31.8	34.0	29.2	13.4	15.1	14.3
Employment (Million)	70.6	90.4	7.2	7.2	12.3	14.7

Source: National Survey Organisation

Women informal labourers work in the subsistence agriculture, as seasonal workers in plantations, or at home, often for extremely low wages. The dominance of primary sector in rural areas and other sectors in urban areas for employment of women is evident from the Table—5. Nevertheless, it is women who make a major contribution to family income. The reasons for this discrepancy are their low formal education and training as compared to men, the traditional allocation of roles and limitations of formal labour market for women (Table—6). Besides because of mechanization and modernisation in agriculture and high technological basis of formal labour markets, the influx labour force has no other than to work in the informal sector.[8]

Informal sector gives some type of relief in the form of readymade jobs to the people, thereby help a greater extent in removing the seasonal unemployment among the agricultural labourers, marginal and poor farmers. The incomes in the informal employment in this sector are for better than in the rural areas. Children, handicapped and maimed are found in this sector. But they are not likely to be employed by the formal sector, which forbids employment of children below certain age, lays down strict conditions for appointment of women and required level of formal training.[9]

Women labourers who face difficulties is obtaining employment in organised industries, government departments, are employed in the informal sector, as contribution labourers, part time domestic servants, casual workers in mills and child attendants in different middle class families.

Comparatively higher incidence of home-based work amongest women can be analysed by domestic responsibilities, child bearing and realising and absence of other adults in the family. This is evident particularly in case of poor women who are movable to hire domestic help and are constrained to take up home-based work though it is less remunerative.[10]

The activity status classification in the traditional censuses and labour force surveys distinguishes between the self 'employee' and employees. In India the employee are further split in to 'regular' and 'casual' workers. There has been a decline in the proportion of self-employed workers, in agriculture as also non-agriculture, in rural and urban areas in India, Except among men in the urban area (Table—8).[11]

Among 'employees' there was an increase in the number of casual workers among both men and women. Among 'regular' workers, however, there was a small increase in the proportion of women in various areas, whereas there was decline in the number of male workers in both rural and urban areas.[12]

Table—6
Distribution of Women Employment by Board Economic Sectors

Sectors	*Rural*			*Urban*		
	1973	*1983*	*1991*	*1973*	*1983*	*1991*
Primary	89.9	87.8	85	33.5	31.7	25.3
Secondary	5.7	7.1	8.0	28.3	30.1	31.2
Tertiary	4.4	5.1	7.0	38.2	38.2	43.5
Total	**100.00**	**100.00**	**100.00**	**100.00**	**100.00**	**100.00**

Source: National Sample Survey Organisation

Table—7
Educational Composition of Working Women

Educational level	*1997-78*		*1987-88*	
	Rural	*Urban*	*Rural*	*Urban*
Illiterate	89.5	65.2	82.9	54.6
Primary Literate	8.7	17.5	12.1	19.4
Middle	1.1	4.7	3.1	6.6
Secondary	0.6	7.6	1.6	10.9
Graduate and Above	0.1	5.0	0.3	8.4
Total	**100.00**	**100.00**	**100.00**	**100.00**

Source: National Sample Survey Organisation

Table—8
Employment Status of Workers(Percentage)

	Male			*Female*		
Rural	*Self Employed*	*Regular Employed*	*Casual Employed*	*Self Employed*	*Regular Employed*	*Casual Employed*
1977-78	62.8	10.6	26.6	62.1	2.8	35.1
1983		10.3	29.2	61.9	2.8	35.3
1987-88	58.6	10.0	31.4	60.8	3.7	35.5
1993-94	57.9	8.3	33.8	58.5	2.8	38.8
Urban						
1977-78	40.4	46.4	13.2	49.5	24.9	25.6
1983	49.9	43.7	15.4	45.8	25.8	28.4
1987-88	41.7	43.7	14.6	47.1	27.2	24.4
1993-94	41.7	42.1	16.2	45.4	28.6	26.0

Survey: NSSO, Survakshana, various issues

The Plight of Informal Women Labourers

Women who originate from the poorer sections of the society have some common characteristics. There features can be summoned up as inadequate opportunities to work, greater impact of unemployment, underemployment and casual nature of work, greater vulnerability because of lack of education and skill, lesser mobility, a systematic social custom of under-rating women's work and lack of access to better technologies, tools and productive assets. To considerable extent, poor women keep moving between the status of self employed, casual labour and unemployed.

The vast majority of rural women in the unorganized sector are landless who work in the fields, look after animals, involve in food production, food processing, forestry and rural industry. They also participate in construction work, engage in factories, work in mines and engage in trade and vending. Besides, they also bear the burden of children, collection of firewood and water, which pressurize their time and energy. Environmental degradation like deforestation and commercialization of forest resources, indiscriminate tapping of ground water resources have further aggravated women's problems. Growing agricultural poverty has led many male members to migrate in search of work, leaving their families behind to face the consequences. Moreover, the increasing pauperization in rural areas has led to streams of migration and polarization between rural and urban areas with considerable concentration of wealth and social services in the urban economy.

There have been migrants because of displacement by development projects of irrigation, industries etc., which influence women substantially. If the male member migrates the female member shoulders the total responsibility for the family left behind. If the entire family migrates, women themselves confront the problems of performing the dual role of earner and home-worker while living and working in conditions which lack even the basic sanitary facilities. Even the women suffer exploitation at the hands of the contractors in construction and brick-kiln industry and have to move from place to place in search of employment.

United Nations Women's Conference

The United Nations Women's Conference achieved two breakthroughs as it endeavoured to remove some of the lingering issues bogging down on a 10 year blue print on women's rights.

Islamic conservatives agreed to compromise which ended a deadlock on inheritance rights for girls while industrialized nations bended off footing the bill for the blue print or platform for action.

The breakthroughs came in hurried emergency sessions aimed at overcoming contentious issues holding in progress at the United Nations fourth world women's conference in Beijing 1995.

Opponents say many countries could lite cultural differences as a loophole to avoid conforming to the conference's draft platform for action.

Wrangling between conservative Islamic nations, spearheaded by Iran and Sudan, and Western Governments had bagged the biggest UN international conference.

UNDP's Human Development report, 1994 says "Despite all over technological breakthrough we still live in a world where a fifth of the developing world's population goes hungry every might, a quarter lacks access to even basic necessities like safe drinking water and a third lives in a state of object despair at such a margin of human existence that words fails to describe it." Needless to say, the most alarming implication is that women get more and more marginalised in the struggle for survival among those living in poverty where resources are unevenly distributed. As a result, the development process has emphasised on women.

In agriculture, mining, industry and other related works, there has been a decline in women's employment. This decline has been due to several factors. These are prohibition on underground and hazardous works, introduction of labour saving devices, technological improvements in methods of production, rise in the wage rate of women. In addition to there, employment of women results in extra burden on the employers on account of statutory requirement of provisions concerning women labourers.

Informal women labourers' employment is mainly concentrated in unskilled or a few semi-skilled jobs where simple or traditional skills are required. The high rate of illiteracy among women, lack of skill and professional training, absence of on the job training facilities and prevalent social attitudes towards their employment are some of the impediments in the employment of women at the highest levels of production. Moreover, one of the striking features of informal women labourers is their employment on unskilled jobs as they usually shift from one unskilled job to another.

Women Labour in Mining

Nearly 80 per cent of women labourers in the selected small mines in the informal sector belonged to the group "Production and related workers." Most of them are unskilled. As high as 80 per cent of women employed labourers are found unskilled while the semi-skilled labour constitute only 20 per cent. However, in coal and mica mines and subsidiary activities, a majority of women labourers are found to be engaged on semi-skilled jobs like wagon loading, quarry work, black supplying and ore dressing. The proportion of women labourers engaged in supervisory capacity are found to be negligible.

It has been observed that skilled workers constitute large proportion in the mechanized and semi-mechanized mines.

The practice of recruitment of casual labour has been prevalent in all the mines excepting stone, limestone and dolomite mines. Some women labour in organised coal mines are found to be holding, casual status even after completing several years of their services. A large number of women labourers in the mines are temporarily appointed.

Study conducted by Dr.* Behera in Keonjhar district of Orissa mainly Bolani, Joda, Bansapani, Thakurani, Gandhamardan regions pertaining to the iron ore, manganese and chromite mines has brought to light many interesting findings.

---

* Behera, Surendranath., *Mining Labourers in Tribal Belts—A Case Study of Keonjhar District, Orissa* in S. N. Tripathy (Edited) Tribal Labour in India (1997), Mohit Publication, New Delhi

The study reveals that there is larger concentration of younger miners, both male and female in the age of 20-40. Female labourers constitute 32.7 per cent of the total working force among the sample labourers. The hard working nature and economic forces induce a higher participation rate among large number of tribal women. But the percentage of women labourers has been declining in mechanised and semi-mechanised mines like Joda Iron ore, Joda West Manganese under TISCO, Bolani Iron ore under SAIL and Baula Chromite (underground) under FACOR. As has been pointed out earlier, the decline in the employment of women labourers may be due to the ban imposed by the Government on the employment of women for underground work, mechanical works and night shift works. Semi-skilled labour force working in open cast mines and below ground in digging and raising, operations.

It has been observed that though the systems of direct recruitment of labourers are in vogue but mostly the labourers employed through same intermediaries in the organised mining sector.

In mines, absenteeism among women labourers is slightly higher than their male counterparts.

Women labourers are generally found as efficient as their male counterparts. In certain light jobs women labourers are found more proficient requiring higher skill, strength and strenuous work, they are regarded as less proficient by the employers.

Even in organised sector, majority of women labourers as has been observed, are employed in coal, stone, limestone and dolomite at piece rated wages. The periodicity of wage payment was monthly or weekly as has been manifested in most cases.

The average minimum and maximum daily wage rates of both male and female workers are the highest in coal followed by limestone and dolomite and iron ore mines.

Living Conditions of Women

In the un-organised sector, in most of the mines, women were working only in shift and that too during day time. Multiple shift system for women labourers is in operation only in limited mines.

Latrine and urinals in most of the units are not in sanitary condition and has no proper arrangements for supply of water and lacks sufficient room for their improvement.

As the mine workers are working in an atmosphere of dust and heat, it is essential to ensure provisions of washing facilities separate for men and women.

An Overview of the Analysis

Wage employment of women in Industry is not a new phenomenon. In fact, ever since the advent of the Industrial Revolution rural women were encouraged to leave their villages and take up paid employment in mines and informal sectors. Notwithstanding the fact that women have been working in such mining and plantation activities, their living conditions are most deplorable. Besides in unorganised sector, working under most inhuman conditions, they are deprived of same essential benefits like maternity protection, separate toilets and child-care services. Employers do exploit the weak bargaining power of women labourers by making lower payment of wages compared to their male counterparts.

In the wake of independence and planned policy of industrialisation, though adequate provisions have been made but they are only confined to big mines and factories. Of course, though there exists legislative provisions of regularising the working condition of women, ensuring provision of welfare amenities and protecting them from health hazards and economic exploitation but unfortunately, there lacks effective implementation in case of small mining operations. Efforts for tackling numerous complex problems of informal women labourers have been handicapped by absence of reliable statistical data relating to their income and living conditions.

With regard to living conditions of women labourers as early as in 1953 the Labour Bureau made a study and the report was brought to light entitled, "Economic and social status of women workers in India." The report was confined to important industries like cotton, jute textiles and coal mining etc.

Subsequently, in 1958, the Labour Bureau and Planning Commission jointly made a study entitled, "Women in employment (1901-1956)". In the year 1964 a publication entitled 'Women in Employment' and in the year 1975 'Women in Industry' were released by the Labour Bureau. Of course, these studies were relating to women labourers in mines, factories and plantations where the Acts like Mines Act 1952, the Factories Act 1948 and Plantation Labour Act 1951 are applicable. But in case of small mining operations mainly undertaken by contractors and private employers, more specifically informal sector, such studies have not yet been conducted extensively.

Inspite of the fact that women are accepting wage employment at an increasing rate, their mainstay continues to be agriculture. The proportion of women employed in mining and quarrying was 0.40 per cent during 1971 has declined to 0.35 per cent and 0.31 per cent during 1981 and 1991, respectively.

A perusal of our analysis brought to light that the labour laws are exclusively applicable to organised sectors where as in small mines and other activities employers mainly private persons do not adhere to such laws. Further, it has been demonstrated that women labourers participated the male folk in household cultivation and handicraft industry. Women labourers have helped by performing multi-dimensional activities. Their activities range from agricultural activities support to household art, craft, designing of pottery, weaving of clothes, etc. Thus, mainly women contribute in the economic support of the household mainly by working at their homes or by nearby farms. However, with the rapid growth of population, industrialisation modernisation, urbanisation, decline in the household industries, growing economic needs and social awakening, the women do participate out side their homes in various activities. Thus, women labourers do work in non-traditional activities outside their villages and geographical boundaries. The increasing economic necessities have forced them to co-operate and support the male members for supplementing the family income. In certain cases due to displacement of male bread earner or death of the husband the women have to toil hard for the upbringing of dependent children. Such women-headed households mainly employed in informal sector activities.

It is pertinent to mention that the Department of Women and child, Government of India constituted a National Commission on Self-employed Women and Women in Internal Sector in 1987. The Commission was mainly to make a comprehensive study of the status of the self-employed women and women in informal sector and to suggest measures to improve the conditions of their work, wages and work situations. The Commission, as part of their responsibility, conducted a limited sample survey of women workers in poverty and accumulated a wealth of first hand information on the subject.

Similarly, the National perspective plan for women 1988-2000 prepared by the core group set-up by the Government also documented the contribution of women in the informal sector. It estimated that 94 per cent of the workers in the informal sector are women.

Contribution of the Informal Sector

As regards the contribution of the informal sector to employment of the country, the 1981 census reveals that the informal sector provides employment to about 42.76 million women works force. These women are distributed among light major economic activities. They are as follows:

Agriculture (1.87 million), dairying (75 million), fishing (1 million), Small animal husbandry (1.5 million), Khadi and Village Industry (1.70 million), Handlooms (2.98 million), Handicrafts (0.54 million) and in sericulture (1.30 million) of the village and small industries Sector.

As regards the contribution of informal sector in terms of income, the limited data on the subject indicates that goods worth Rs. 11,590.00 crores were produced in 1990 under the four major occupations of Khadi and Village Industry, Hnadlooms, Handicrafts and Sericulture. Of which, production worth Rs 3,271.90 crores was meant for exports. If we consider the source of income from one single occupation viz. handicrafts where women are dominating, then it was Rs. 5400 crores during 1998-99, as projected (T. K. Sarojini, "Sensitising Census Enumerators", Social Welfare, August-September 1995).

Rural Women Employment

Several efforts have been made to improve the economic status of the rural women by providing them employment opportunities. But all such endeavours have not brought desired results. The key to better employment is the education of women and diversification of opportunities supported either by Government projects or by private investors. Government through its plans and policies can empower women by ensuring employment and raising income levels. To ensure the benefits to the rural women, the administrative machinery has to be more vigilant towards security of employed women in rural areas.

But unfortunately, in most of the Government sponsored projects as has been observed (Employment Assurance Scheme, JRY and others) substantial proportion of the investible resources are either mis-utilised or mis-appropriated. Such leakages of fund reduces the investible resources and thereby the generation of employment and increase of income can not take place. Thus, removal of poverty remains a distant dream. Corruption eats away the vitals of economy and as such a parallel economy (block money) is created constituting about 40% of the national income. Therefore, there is urgent need of fixing responsibility or accountability to different plan implementors or executors. Obviously, there should be suitable legislative measures and changes in the constitution to provide it within one power by which it can not be treated as 'toothless of paper tiger'.

The constitution guarantees certain rights and privileges, to women through the fundamental rights and Directive Principle of State Policy. Article 14 confers on men and women equal right and opportunities in the political economic and social spheres. Article 15 prohibits, discrimination against any citizen on the grounds of religion, race, caste and sex etc. Article 15(3) contains an enabling provision for the state to make affirmative discrimination in favour of women. Article-16 provides for equality of opportunity in matter of public appointments for all citizens. Article 39(e) ensures equal pay for equal work and article 42 directs the state to make provisions for ensuring just and humane conditions of work and maternity relief.

Ironically, most of the women in rural India, are employed as agricultural labourers in construction works and largely depend on contractors for their employment who usually exploit them. Children their wages would account for upto half of national income. Unfortunately, lot of women in our country still remain pitiful due to non-recognition of their work in development. Thus, it is recognised that women's contribution is found in two important fields—household activities and in agriculture or related primary employment. But the pressing problems faced by women are health and education, malnutrition and child bearing have been playing havoc with the health status of women ultimately, affect the economic activity as well as their participation in income generating activities.

Women's Education

With regard to education opportunities for women's education has been an important component of national endeavour. Despite these efforts, gender disparity persist with uncompromising tenacity, move so in rural areas and among disadvantaged communities. In order to neutralise the accumulated distortions of the past, there will be a well-conceived edge in favour of women. The national education system will play a positive, interventionist role in the empowerment of women. The removal of women's illiteracy and obstacles inhibiting their access to, and intention in elementary education will receive over-riding priority through provision of special support services, setting of time targets and effective monitoring.

Apart from the direct developmental benefit of education for women, improvements in overall social and economic indices smaller families and reduced infant mortality, improved quality of life, enhanced economic productivity and improvement in family health are some of the other benefits associated with education of women.

Exploitation of Rural Women

The rural women in our society are exploited and denied their basic rights. Their inherent dignity and equal inalienable rights are not recognised in the society. The socio-economic status and the nature and mode of work have changed alongwith the new developments in the society. Today, there is hardly any place and work inside or outside home where a women can not perform. But the society, particularly, rural society is not still ready to accept any change in women's role work position and status because of the orthodox and conservative belief rampant in villages (Dr. S. Meharaj Begum, "Women Rights and Rural Employment" Kurukshetra, April 2000 p.62)

Despite constitutional safegrards, legislative measures, package of programmes by the Government no significant development has been witnessed in the rural India. The plans and programmes could not bring any tangible changes in the socio-economic conditions rather aggravated the situation by widening the gap between the 'rich' and the 'poor'. This may due to loopholes in the plan implementation by which the benefits could not be percolated at the grass-root level. One of the potentially effective methods of guaranteeing the women for their employment is to educate them, to create awareness among them and finally encourage their participation in rural workers' organisation. But all these can be effectively implemented when the defaulters or dishonest officials or agencies are penalised or punished by law which in turn requires a drastic change in the constitutional provision and dedicated officials. The administrative un-preparedness and lack of political will stand in the way to effective implementation of plans and programmes aiming at the well-being of the rural women in our country.

Finally, it can be concluded that the development of our country is intrinsically linked to the social, economic and political empowerment of our people especially women. Ensuring gender equality by removing gender discrimination mainly among the marginalised, unprotected, unorganized and informal women labourers is the key to real empowerment.

Moreover, the sustainable development of an economy is intricately related to empowerment of women. Progress of women can only ensure steady economic growth. Discrimination against women is incompatible with human dignity which impedes the full realisation of the potentialities of women. When the creative abilities and personal contribution of half the population are subject to constant subjugation, socio-economic progress is bound to be jeopardized.

The first and foremost feature towards empowering women is to allow them availing their basic human right to education. The social returns of women's education go far beyond individual welfare, it acts as an agent of national development through improvement in the standard of health and hygiene, reduction in child mortality rate, increase in labour productivity decline in fertility rate, greater political empowerment and improved sense of nationality.

To remove gender disparities in education, the Jontien Declaration suggested a seven point agenda, which include:

(i) Enactment of compulsory primary education laws and penalties for non-enrolment of girls as severe as at boys;

(ii) Reduction in the grants by the Central Government and any other funding agencies to the State Government and NGO's for education in proportion to the prevalent disparity in the enrolment of boys and girls;

(iii) Overcoming the supply-side obstacles by creating schools within easily reach of the community, by establishing single sex schools, by providing scholarships to the girls etc;

(iv) Provision of non-female teachers;

(v) Increase in the community participation in planning and management of the schools;

(vi) To enhance the overall status of women in the society.

Developing countries primarily through empowering of women have achieved remarkable progress in terms of literacy, health and economic well-being of families. Hence, there is a need to actively promote women's access to quality education, credit health care, employment and social security. But these alturistic objectives can be achieved only through the effective implementation of anti-corruption acts by nationalising the properties of corrupted politicians, officials and administrative authorities. Moreover, protecting the rights of women and the girl child, ensuring their status by ending practices and customs which perpetuate gender discrimination and finally, formulating policy safeguarding the interests of women workers, unorganised labourers, marginalised female bread earners and millions of tribals of India is the need of the hour. A package of security measures, social security safetynets are not only to be introduced but should also be implemented in order to provide strong and effective reliefs to the depressed and down-trodden, poverty stricken sections of the society.

The plight of the female-headed households, displaced tribals, informal women labourers are heart-rendering and therefore, should be redressed by enforcement of suitable laws which combat and curb corruption.

A personal of the study boils down that since women's development is directly related with national development, the effective management and development of women's resources i.e., their abilities, interests, skills and other potentialities are of paramount importance for the mobilisation and development of human resources. In VI five year plan a special chapter has been added "Women and Development" in which it has been mentioned in its strategy that the main drawbacks in women's development have been mainly pre-occupation with repeated pregnancies without respite in physical work, lack of education both formal and non-formal, a pre-dominance of social prejudices along with lack of independent income generation activity or independent assets. The strategy for socio-economic development must encompass the development of education, employment and health which are inter-dependent and dependent on the total development process.

In the context of economic development, the strategy for rural development which seeks to improve the standard of living of the poor by increasing the productivity and income generation of women-headed households.

The Unbearable Burden

The women involved in home-based economic activities and cattlecare, the limitation of space makes their conditions worse at times bordering on a sub-human level with women, children and animals sleeping in the same area with little of no ventilation. Some women come to live permanently while others come during the agricultural off season but they all face a shortage of hcusing facilities and other civic amenities. The migratory labour position is worse as the demand of work compels them to move from place to place. Women living in urban slums, face greater difficulties than in rural areas, largely because of the terrible over-crowding, lack of privacy and lack of essential services (for which they are entirely dependent of civic authorities).

Access to resources such as land, credit, technology and training has always been difficult for women. Since always all farm extension workers are men the needs of women for upgrading their skills is often overlooked. Social segregation of the sexes further discourages contract between women farmers and male extension agents.

Women are seen as indirect beneficiaries and not as participants or target groups. This discrimination exists in spite of the fact that most of these jobs are less paying and usually the most menial of jobs in every sector are performed by women. It has also been observed that women are being increasingly displaced from even these most unproductive and low paid job opportunities. This is because of the structural problems that have arisen in the rural informal sectors as a result of the land ownership and land use pattern the nature of land and power relations in rural areas and the gender division of labour.

In the urban informal sector women work as petty traders and producers selling and producing a wide variety of goods such as vegetables, fruits, flowers, cooked food or groceries etc., or as domestic labour. In both the rural and urban areas they are engaged as construction workers. In addition, women spend on an average 6/7 hours a day on domestic chores as well as collection of fuel, fodder and water and on childcare.

Employment of women in the rural unorganised sector can be categorised into nine main heads. These are agriculture, dairy, small animal husbandry, fishery, social and agro-forestry, khadi and village industries, handlooms and handicrafts and agriculture. To boost productivity of these sectors provisions of investment outlays are made through government programmes. But the programmes are executed largely by male decision makers and extension workers.

Working in harsh sub-human conditions of starvation and squalor, occupations in this sector and equally characterized by low wages and low capital formation. Workers are often left without a permanent trading place or technical devices. The problem of women relates to that of access to markets, materials and credit but also of problems that arise from the fact that these women are most often enmeshed in the complex web of other exploitative structures such as middlemen, merchants, contractors and money lenders.[13]

The problems of piece rate work is not only the question of low wages but also discriminatory wages, as the nature of the work is home based-especially when it involves the entire families labour of both women and children (weaning and beedi rolling), which often turns out to be in the nature of unpaid labour.

Women and the Policy of Economic Reforms

The new macro economic policies that are being implemented in India are likely to have a major impact on the lives and work of women. Although a detailed analysis of the impact is difficult at present especially due to lack of gender disagreed data, some researchers feel that their policies lead to greater unemployment especially among women. As structural adjustment squeezes women out of jobs and pares down services provided by the state, it is likely that a greater number of women will be pushed into providing such services by taking up informal employment. At the same time inflation will reduce the purchasing power of the "working poor" forcing women into an ever-increasing multiplicity of roles.

Women in the informal sector most often live and work at home or outside under constant threat of loosing their job with no viable alternatives, increasingly forced to cater to unstable workers such as export market and handicraft production. The imposition of wage valuation by the dominant patriarchal culture pushes women to a position of subordination, subject to discrimination not only at home but also in the labour market.[14]

Thus, this traditional/culture dimension is reflected in the assignment of work roles for women of the informal sector markets which has been offered by the trade unions. Living in the shadow of the colonial past, Indian trade unions of the organised sector do not lend any solidarity to these informal sector workers. Although dealing only with 10 per cent of the working population, these organised sector unions still object to the recognition of the informal sector workers.[15]

Informal Sector and Liberalisation

The policy of liberalisation has put contradictory demands on labour. On the one hand unionisation of labour is considered to have grown very strong, impeding the progress of liberalisation. This has led to moves combating the power of labour such as amendments to the Industrial Dispute Act, and other. On the otherhand, labour is seen as weak and exploited experiencing adverse impact of liberalisation. Therefore, there are more demands for adequate protection of labour, construction workers, agricultural labour and domestic servants.

This anomalous situation has emerged because labour is now divided into two categories 'organised'—which is strongly protected by laws having their vociferous trade unions and unorganised labour—which is unprotected, doubly exploited, and rarely organised. Unorganised or informal sector constituting more than 90 per cent of work force remain uncovered by protective legislation and therefore pose a serious problem as it is deprived of the benefits of liberalisation. In fact, the working population, specifically the informal women labourers would suffer the detrimental impact in terms reduced wages, unemployment and destruction of traditional social safety.[16]

Ironically, the problem of widening of inequality between the two components of workforce, has attracted little attention of the political leaders or economic planners.

In the light of the above stated analysis, it is pertinent to suggest that the government should recognize the various problems of informal sector workers and establish clear cut labour standards. Representatives of informal sector must be included in the trade delegations of tripartite meetings and also in labour delegations to ILO and other international labour meetings. Notwithstanding these, there seems no significant shift in policy of the government nor also in the policy of Central trade unions to extend solidarity to the workers of informal sector.[17]

Class Oppressions

Dispossession of assets, insufficient means of subsistence, degrading living conditions etc. are factors responsible for keeping the poor women in the web of poverty and acute powerlessness.

In the case of women workers, the complete lack of assets amidst in landed gentry, along with irregular nature of agricultural wage labour and powerlessness of the women have always altered the terms and conditions of employment. Lack of protective legislation for women is the result of both apathy and vested interests in perpetuating this system. The landed gentry's control over the rural policy has further prevented the enforcement of reform/legislation for these women. Additionally, poor rural women are essentially excluded from the land reform programme. Not only the husband invariably receive the land title, the women has no legal rights over land use, property disposal, or access to benefits from land's use. Lacking awareness of their political and natural rights, women workers still continue the drudgery of their daily labour.[18]

The poor women are having no other option but to borrow from the 'moneylenders' or 'village landlord's. This indigenous system is such a disastrous system itself operating on exorbitant rates of interest that the poor enmesh themselves in continued indebtedness resulting in vicious circle of poverty.

In most cases, the poor pawned their land, house, jewels and small assets to such moneylenders in order to borrow at a high rate of interest which ultimately forced them into perpetual debt.[19]

Further it has been observed that decline in the forest area due to shifting cultivation, restrictions imposed by the government in the use of forest, lavish expenditure for social ceremonies, disease and indebtedness are factors which entangle the tribal agricultural women in the web of mystery and perpetual poverty. Thus, the unorganised tribal women are in the midst of indebtedness and maintain a sub-human living.[20]

In the wake of liberalisation and privatisation policy adopted by the government, it is the informal sector which faces the great stress and strain. Because the market forces of price regulation operate to induce investment in the profit-oriented, low-cost goods. The lure of profit induces to modernise the economy through the use of modern and upgraded equipments both in farm and non-farm sectors of the economy. Thus, there is every possibility of technological upgradation leading to structural unemployment and replacement of labourers especially, informal women labourers.[21]

The foregoing analysis brought to limelight that women play a crucial and significant role in economic development of a country. But there is no denying the fact that women have suffered utter neglect and deprivation over centuries. Despite their significant contribution to the economy, they have been sidetracked in the economic estimation of their contribution. Women are mostly employed in the informal sector in diversified activities.

New economic policy and globalisation has little prospects for the informal women labour as they are not covered by protective legislation.

REFERENCE

1. Becker, Gary S. *"The Economics of Discrimination"*(1957), University of Chicago Press
2. Arrow, Kenneth, *"Models of Rule Discrimination and Some Mathematical Models of Rule Discrimination"*.
3. Mincer, U.J. and S. Polachek, *"Family Investment in Human Capital: Earnings of Women"* (1972) Journal of Political Economy, Vol. 82, No. 2
4. Polachek S. *"Discontinuities in Labour Force Participation and its Effect on Women's Market Earnings* (1975), C.B.L Wood(Ed) *"Sex Determination and the Division of Labour"* Columbia University Press, New York
5. Stiglitz, J.F. *"Approaches to the Economics of Discriminations,"* American Economics Review, May 1973

6. Madden J.F. "*The Economics of Sex Discrimination*, Lexington, Books, Lexington, Mass, 1973

7. Meher Raj Kishore '*The Migrant Female Bread Winners: Women in the Informal Secondary Sector of Rourkela, Orissa*' (1994) The Indian Journal of Labour Economics, Vol. 37 No. 3

8. Yadav, Ravi Prakash., *Women Workers World-wide* (1999) Social Welfare, August p. 4.

9. Tripathy, S.N. (Dr.) and Das, Soudamini (1991), *Informal Women Labour in India*. Op. Cit, p-7.

10. Pathak, Pushpa and Patnaik, *India's Lowest Range of the Production Process: Women Home-Based Piece-rate Workers in Urban India* (1994), The Indian Journal of Labour Economics, Vol. 37 No. 3 p. 469.

11. Unni, Jeemol and Ravi Kumar, *Informal Sector: Women in the Emerging Labour Market*, Op. Cit p. 629.

12. *Ibid* p. 630.

13. P. Thippaiah, *Women Workers in Urban Unorganised Sector* (1989) Social Welfare May pp. 21-22.

14. Ammanchalar, Jaya., *Women in the Informal Sector: Need for Policy Option*, Op. Cit p. 41

15. *Ibid* p. 68.

16. Bhatt, Ela R., *The Unprotected Labour* (1994) The Indian Journal of Labour Economics, Vol 37 No. 3, p. 6448.

17. Ammanchalar, Jaya

18. *Ibid* p. 69.

19. *Ibid* p. 70.

20. Tripathy S.N. (Dr.) *Central Labour in Agricultural Sector* (2000), New Delhi, Discovery Publishing House, p. 47.

21. *Ibid*.

Chapter—3

A Profile of the Study Area

This Chapter intends to the socio-economic and demographic profile of the Berhampur City, the area of the study. The profile of the area gives a picture regarding the nature of the setup from which the sample households are selected for the purpose of field study.

Geographical Location of the District Ganjam

Ganjam is one of the southern districts of Orissa with 100 kms. of coastal line. The district ranks third in respect of population. It falls on Calcutta-Madras National Highway No. 5 and is surrounded by the Boudh-Kandhamala (Phulbani) and Puri district in the north, Srikakulam district of Andhra Pradesh in south, Bay of Bengal and Puri district in the east.

Historical Background of Berhampur City

Brahmapur, later misspelt as Berhampur by the English, was a prominent centre of trade, traffic and culture by the time it became the political headquarters of the Mahuri estate which was founded by the local chieftain allowed by Purusottam Dev, the Suryavansi Gajapati King of Orissa during 15th century A.D.

Berhampur was a prominent town in the Golakunda Muslim State from 1571 till 1667, and in Nizam's State of Hyderabad from 1667 till 1753. It was also an important centre of trade and power under the authority of the French from 1753 till 1759 and it remained as an important town of Ganjam under the Madras presidency from 1766 till 1936, during the rule of East India Company and the British Crown.

The chief industry in Berhampur was the weaving of tassar silk which was manufactured into gold embroidered turbans, dresses and other articles of weaving apparel. These were of excellent quality. Such silken and cotton products of the town were adjusted as excellent products in the exhibitions held in London (1860s).

"The ordinary artisans at Berhampur on a class were very indifference set of workmen and they took little pride in their work. The bazaars were well supplied with ordinary necessities of life. During the winter times English vegetables such as peas, beans, canilis and potatoes could be produced with great success."[1]

Demographic Profile

The decadal variations in rural population in 1961, 1971, and 1981 are 15.10, 20.84 and 12.16 per cent respectively. Table—9 demonstrates that the percentage of the rural population to the total population is falling gradually. The percentage of the ubran population to the total population is 14.25 per cent as per 1991 census and as such it occupies the fourth position in Orissa. This percentage is higher than the all Orissa figure of 11.79.

Sex Ratio in India, Orissa and Ganjam

The sex ratio is taken as the number of females per thousand males. In 1991, sex ratio in India was 929:1000. The census figure since 1901 show a successive decline in sex ratio except in the year 1951 and 1981 when it registered an increase by a unit of one and four respectively while in 1991, it decreased by 5 points. In 1901, the sex ratio was 971 (Table—4.2) and it stood at 946 in census year of 1951. The maximum decline for 11 points) occurred between 1961 and 1971, when sex ratio decreased from 941 to 930.

Table—9
Decadal Variation in Sex Ratio of India

Census year	*Sex Ratio (female per thousand and males)*
1901	972
1911	964
1921	955
1931	950
1941	945
1951	946
1961	941
1971	930
1981	934
1991	929

Source: Census of India, 1991, Government of India

The district of Ganjam is rich in water, land forest and mineral resources. It has developed transport and communication network. The district is industrially backward. The backward population (Scheduled Caste and Scheduled Tribe) of the undivided district constitutes almost one fourth of the total population. The majority of population depends directly or indirectly on agriculture. The rate of female literacy is low. There is rapid growth of urban population in the district even though there has not been a sound industrial development so far.

Agricultural Scenario

It is believed that the word "Ganjam" has been derived from the Persian word 'Ganj-I-am' which means the granary of the world. This highlights the importance of agriculture in the district that covers variety of both kharif and rabi crops. It has got potential for the expansion of food-processing industry.

Area Sown

The total geographical area of the undivided district is 1220 thousand hectares. The net area sown comes to 41 per cent and it is followed by forests spreading over 47 per cent of the total area. The areas sown more than once cover and 70 per cent of the net area sown during the year 1980-1981 and it which is showing the increasing trend from year to year.

Irrigational Network

Timely and assured availability of water to crops is the key factor for increasing agricultural production. The area under irrigation from major and medium irrigation projects comprises 37 per cent of the total irrigated area, where as the area under minor irrigation projects covered only two per cent of the total irrigated area in the year 1980-81. During 1980-81 the total area irrigated by all projects kharif and rabi where 270.857 hectares. The Rushikulya reservoirs, Baghua and Ghodahada dams are the main dam projects of this district. Harabhangi and Daha projects are going to be completed in a short period of time. Both these projects are being financed by the World Bank.

Principal Crops

The principal crops of the district are paddy, ragi, mung, biri, til, groundnut, kulthi sugarcane and chilly. Usually paddy is sown (by way of broadcasting) on rainfed lands and transplanted on irrigated and rainfed medium and low lands. Next to paddy, ragi is the most important crop. It is grown 2 to 3 times during a year. Sugarcane is grown in and around Aska and Paralakhemundi abundantly. During rabi season mung and biri are grown in large area. Groundnut is grown both during kharif and rabi seasons. The area under rice is the largest among all the crops which the district produces.

Size of Land Holdings

As per 1976-77 agricultural census the number of land holdings in the district was 3.56 lakh and the area operated by the above holdings was 3.77 lakh hectares. A study on different classes of holdings revealed that 66.9 per cent of the total holdings come under the size group of less than one hectare, followed by the size group of 1 to 1.99 hectares according for 9.3 per cent of the same. The rate of 13.8 came under 2 hectares. The remaining 13.8 per cent of the holdings come under the size group of 2 to 10 hectares and above.

The River System

The important rivers of the district (undivided) are Rushikulya, Bada Nadi, Mahendra Tanaya, Bansadhara, Hada Bhanga, Ghodahada, Dhanei and Baghua. The largest river Rushikulya is about 160 kms long. It originates from Daringibadi in Baliguda of Phulbani and is joined by Bada Nadi at Aska and enters in the Bay of Bengal at Ganjam. The Ghodahada river is the chief tributary of Rushikulya.

Economic Minerals and Industries

The major economic minerals of the district are clay limestone, manganese, monazites and black granite materials etc. Along with Ganjam coast illuminate, monozite, zircum and granite talc occur only in R. Udayagiri area.

The coastal sand of Bay of Bengal at Gopalpur-on-Sea contains rare-earth minerals such as illuminite, silimanites, zircon and monozite. The I.R.E. of Government of India is an important public undertaking operating near Chatrapur of Ganjam. In the district I.R.E. has given employment to 1200 persons. In 1991 I.R.E. has commissioned a Thorium Plant as its sister unit which is an export-oriented plant.

Pisciculture

The district is endowed with 100 kms. long coastal line and salt lake Chilika. The nolias of the costal belt and other professional fishermen depend on fishing in the Bay of Bengal and the Chilika Lake. The other sources of fish in this district are rivers and tanks.

The Administration

The Ganjam District (undivided) has been dived into four Revenue Sub-Divisions, 14 Tehsils and 29 C.D. Blocks. There are 2 Municipalities, 18 N.A.Cs and 20 towns in this district. Berhampur is the Headquarter of the Southern Revenue Division. Chatrapur is the District Headquarter. Since 1993 the district has been divided into Ganjam and Gajapati districts.

Berhampur: The Area of the Sample Study

Berhampur is the Sub-divisional Headquarter and the biggest city of Ganjam. The city is primarily commercial and administrative importance. The present study covers two urban informal sub-sectors construction and domestic households. As many as to women workers in the construction sector and number in the domestic household sector have been selected at random for the purpose of study as explained in the introduction chapter.

Table—10
Decennial Variation in Population of Berhampur Town from 1901 to 1991

Census Year	*Total Population*	*Decenneal Variation in Population*
1901	25,729	-
1911	31,456	22.25
1921	32,731	4.05
1931	37,750	15.33
1941	43,536	15.32
1951	62,343	43.19
1961	76,931	23.39
1971	1,17,662	52.94
1981	1,62,407	38.02
1991	2,10,585	29.66

Source: Statistical Handbook of Ganjam, 1989-90, Census of India 1991 (Provisional)

It is revealed from the Table—10 that during the last decade the population of the city has increased at a rate of 3 per cent per annum approximately and it is likely to increase at this rate.

Table—11
Male and Female Population in Berhampur Town from 1901-1991

Year	*Total Population*	*Total Male*	*Percentage of Males to Total Population*
1901	25729	12163	47.04
1911	31456	15331	48.74
1921	32231	16001	48.89
1931	37750	18490	48.98
1941	43536	21948	50.41
1951	62393	31233	50.10
1961	76931	39890	51.85
1971	117661	60932	51.79
1981	162407	84396	51.96
1991	210585	79510	52.06

Source: District Statistical Handbook of Ganjam, 1980-81.

It is inferred from the Table—11 and 12 that there has been an increasing trend of male population in the Berhampur City. The Sex-ratio is only 922 females per 1000 males as per 1991 census.

Table—12
Sex Ratio in Berhampur Town from 1901 to 1991

Year	*Total Males*	*Per centage of Female To total popualtion*	*No. of Females per 100 males*
1901	13526	59.96	1126
1911	16125	51.26	1052
1921	16730	51.01	1042
1931	19260	51.92	1042
1941	21552	49.59	982
1951	31110	49.96	996
1961	37041	48.15	929
1971	56730	48.21	931
1981	78011	48.03	924
1991	210585	48.00	922

Sources: 1. District Statistical Handbook of Ganjam-1980-81

2. District Statistical Handbook-1991

Further, the Table—12. confirms continuous fall in the female population in comparison to the male population in the city of Berhampur. The decline in the female population comparison to male population in the city can be due to migration of males to the city leaving the females at their home and hearth, unfavourable sex ratio can cause absenteeism, emotional disturbances and low earning to male members living in the city.

Unbalanced sex ratio is neither socially nor economically desirable. However, it can be concluded that the female population in the city is declining due to the greater exodus of the male population to Berhampur.

The foregoing analysis clearly demonstrates that the district Ganjam (Undivided) is one of the Southern Districts of Orissa with a total population of 27.04 lakhs, of which 84 per cent are inhabiting in rural areas. Agriculture is the mainstay of 70 per cent of its population. The district of Ganjam has only three large scale industries. The Indian Rare Earth's, Aska Co-operative Sugar Industries and Jayshree Chemicals, Ganjam. Thus, it has a limited industrial edifice. The informal women labour finds the avenues of employment in various economic enterprises in Berhampur City.

REFERENCES

1. Maltoby., *"Ganjam District Manuals"*, Madras, 1882, p. 47.
2. District Statistical Handbook 1920-91.

   Directorate of Economics and Statistics, Bhubaneswar (Orissa).

Chapter—4

Socio-Economic Features of Informal Women Labourers

This chapter analyses the socio-economic features of informal women labour employed in construction and service sectors on the basis of field data collected through questionnaire method.

Section 'A' focuses on the features of informal women labour employed in the construction sector whereas Section 'B' highlights on women labour employed in different household (service sector).

SECTION—A

Much before the industrial enterprises taking places, construction activities originated in our country. The massive architectural movements scatter all over the country bear the testimony regarding the advanced state of techniques of construction in pre-industrial India.

With the planned economic development launched during five year plans, construction sector mainly in the form of socio-overhead capital (SOC) like road, bridge, building, river dams, railway construction etc., developed by leaps and bounds.

General Features of Construction Sector

The construction sector has remained labour intensive production with low level of mechanisation.

Most of the features of the organisation of the construction sector as well as the work relations are inherited for centuries from a pre-industrial society.

The modern construction sector in public as well as in private enterprises has been the ramification of colonial era. However, some of the basic ingredients has remained more or less same. For instance:

(i) The mason's status as artisans has remained intact even today;

(ii) The head mason or the maistry is a sub-contractor as well as heads a team of construction workers involved in a particular task;

(iii) The maistry usually works with a team of workers of his choice and moves from site to site with more or less the same team;

(iv) The maistry is often, especially in small construction sites, free to choose the way he works, the order in which the work is to be completed etc;

(v) All the jobs are undertaken on a piece-rate basis. A maistry is contracted to complete a piece of work for a certain fixed payment;

(vi) The caste system is still the institution within which apprentices are trained to become skilled workers, carpenters, masons etc. especially in villages and small towns;

(vii) Even in the formal industrial sector, the contractors in major construction sites, both private and public, are mere financiers with no understanding of the production process and labour management. They are considered as implementors of a plan by the main employer. The production in construction sector has been carried out based on subcontract.

The Low Level of Mechanization

The level of mechanization in the construction industry in India has remained low. Wherever some mechanization has taken place it has been only marginal. Besides, the cheap supply labour, a major cause of this low level of mechanization. Mechanization therefore, may not make immediate economic factor. Whatever the reasons, the fact of a low level of mechanization with the retenion of labour intensive processes, makes it even more difficult to integrate the construction industry.

Organisation Labourers and Inherent Problems

The unorganised nature of the construction labour is directly linked to the process of production involved in this industry. In construction, unlike any other type of production, the product of labour remains stationary while the labour moves from site to site, from one employer to another. This is in contrast to any other type of production where the product of labour moves, while the labour forces remain stationary under the same employer. Also, the different stages of construction are undertaken according to piece-rate by different maistries and they engage different groups of labourers. Work is organised into masonry, carpentry, earthwork, concreting, curing, plumbing, painting and electrical work. Each group of workers is required for work at different times depending on the stage of construction. The concreting work for example would require a group of labourers for a single day after which the mason and his group moves to another site in search of construction work. The group moves from one site to another. The burden of finding employment for the group falls squarely on the maistry. These peculiarities in the nature of construction work are some of the cause for the unstable relationship between employer and employee, the insecurity of employment, difficulty in enforcing the existing labour laws and regulations related to this industry and the problems encountered while organizing the labour force.

"In big, construction sites however, the opportunities for continuity of work, both for maistrys and all categories of labourers exist for longer duration. As a result, in big construction sites it is possible to maintain records and ensure proper working conditions for its labourers. In reality, this does not take place. As these big construction sites are in a position to ensure continuous employment for its workers and maistrie's, they use this as a weapon to manoeuvre and exploit the employees. Thus, the opportunity for continuous employment and the insecurity of work go hand in hand in big construction sites. Moreover, the system of sub-contract is a deliberate choice of the formal industrial sector to deny recognition and responsibility towards the labour force.[2]

Thus various factors peculiar to this industry namely high mobility of labour, changing employer-employee relationships and the 'forced labour' type of situations (prevailing in bigger construction sites), post peculiar problems, while attempting to organize the construction labour force. So long as the construction labourers are not unorganized and labour unions are not established it is not possible to change the scenario.[3]

Data on Construction Labour

Reliable data on the number of workers employed in the construction industry are difficult to find out. According to the census data, the growth of the labour force on construction industry indicate a sharp rise from 1871 to 1901. The Twentieth century census data however indicate fluctuations during the first half of the century and increase in their numbers from 1951 onwards.

Table—13 depicts the percentage distribution of main workers by industrial categories during 1981 to 1991 census.

Table—13
Percentage Distribution of Main Workers by Industrial Categories

S.No.	*Industrial Category*	*1981*		*1991*	
		Female	*Male*	*Female*	*Male*
(i)	Cultivation	33.09	43.71	34.22	39.63
(ii)	Agricultural Labourers	46.34	19.57	44.93	21.05
(iii)	Livestock, Forestry, Fishing, Plantation, and allied activities	1.83	2.37	1.60	1.94
(iv)	Painting and Quarrying	0.35	0.63	0.34	0.70
	PRIMARY	81.61	66.28	81.09	63.38

(Contd . . .)

(v)	(a) Manufacturing and processing, servicing and repair in household industries	4.57	3.18	3.53	2.09
	(b) Manufacturing and processing servicing and repair in other than Household Industries	3.6	8.91	3.88	8.89
(vi)	Construction	0.87	1.87	0.66	2.32
	SECONDARY	9.04	13.96	8.07	13.30
(vii)	Trade and Commerce	2.04	7.41	2.26	8.98
(viii)	Transport, storage and communication	0.37	3.36	0.32	3.54
(ix)	Other services	6.94	8.99	8.26	11.80
	TERTIARY	9.35	19.76	10.84	23.32
	ALL	100.00	100.00	100.00	100.00

Source: Registrar General India, Census of India 1991, Final Population Total, Paper 2 of 1992

The data demonstrates that during 1981 census the female per centage was 0.87 which has declined to 0.66 per cent during 1991. This decline in female participation in construction sector may be due to fiscal orientation policy of the Government. To elaborate the point, most of the construction activities of the Central Government or public sectors are undertaken generally in far off places in urban areas to which the male numbers migrate to participate in such activities. The female generally participate in nearby town areas or places near to their villages as they bear more burden of domestic activities along with supplementing the income of the family. However, if we notice the Table—13 item No. ix clearly shows that the percentage of women working "other services" has increased from 6.94 per cent in 1981 to 8.26 per cent in 1991 census.

This other services include domestic work, maid servants and services which the female members can perform near their home site. This increase in percentage of women participation in service sector may be due to migration of male members to urban areas in search of employment, off-farm activities and increased participation of male members in construction activities. This apparent from the Table—13 the percentage of male participation in construction sector has increased from 1.87 to 2.32 during 1981-1991 census period.

Description of Construction Workers in the Early 20th Century

Royal Commission on labour which was instituted "to inquire into and report on the existing conditions of labour in industrial undertakings and plantations in British India, on the health, efficiency and standards of living of the workers and on the relations between the employers and the employed and to make recommendation" enquired labour in to the condition of construction labour employed as casual and contract labour in the construction of railways.

The number of workers employed as contract labour were not known by them. There were no provisions for housing, water supply, and sanitation for contract labour. Fair wages clause did not exist in public contract. The introduction of contract system was found to be the most suitable arrangement for the British which neither wanted to manage the labour process nor be held responsible for the labour force.

Organisation of the Industry

Economic Organisation industry and various types of labour conglomeration for construction activities may broadly be classified as public and private sectors.

In public sector the constructions are undertaken by various departments and authorities of Central and state Government like Public Works Department CPWD, Posts and Telegraphs, HUDCO etc. The construction activities include in its purview roads, bridges, official quarters commercial buildings, houses etc.

Based on investments, the construction activities can be categorised as big, medium and small constructions.

In both public and private sectors, irrespective of size of constructions, the construction industry operates through a system of subcontract which varies depending upon size of construction and sector. The principal employers as well as constructors do not directly involve themselves in organizing the labour process both in public and private sectors.

The contract system with its origin in the colonial period has provided a working method as well as an attitude in the public sector such that the departments have no responsibility towards labour or quality of construction. Thus, the exploitative system of construction works continued for centuries.

The written contracts however is accompanied by conditions most of which harp on quality. The principal employer provides cement and steel while the contractor would procure other construction materials. The works is carried out through subcontract. The conditions of contract stipulate that 10% of the bill could be withheld from payment for a period of time, in order to ascertain the quality of construction. Of course, such cases arise only in case of big constructions of public sector projects.

Similarly there are conditions for contract with respect to labour (apart from the plethora of labour laws which hold both the principal employer and contractor liable). It has been observed that the conditions relating to labour were violated in all works sites in both public sector and constructions in our case study.

In public works department though there are provisions for inspection, with holding of payments by the principal employer in cases of violations of contract conditions, there has never been cases of such action against contractor in spite of blatant violations of contract conditions. The contractors in the private sectors has generally not taken labour license to engage contract labour.

Subcontracting types of Recruitment: General Scenario

In small constructions in the private sector, masonry, carpentry, painting mosaic work etc. were given on piece rate labour contract to maistris. Maistris, who are skilled workers, would bring their groups of skilled and unskilled workers to whom they had to pay time-rated wages. The construction materials would be provided by the owner and the maistry would organise the work, recruit the required number of workers and complete the task. This is the mode of construction, wherein the artesan organises the labour process. For concerting and earthwork either specialized groups would be engaged or the head mason would get additional hands recruited from the market place to carry out the work. Relationship between employer and workers exists for short durations, at most till a particular phase of construction lasts.[4]

In the big and medium sized construction under the contract system, the contractors would provide construction materials but do not organise the labour process. They engaged sub contractors who would recruit labour, carry out and supervise the work.

The big sites had more concreting and earthwork. Therefore, concreting groups were employed. The contractors had brought groups of labourers from rural areas, housed them on site, paid them low wages in order to maximise profits. Such labourers are generally recruited from drought-prone tribal villages of Orissa.

Even in big constructions where labourers are employed by contractors or builders for long duration, it is the subcontractors who organise and supervise the work. There is no direct relation between employer and labourers. Thus, the employer is not responsible for the work of the labourers. The labourers are paid distressed wages, discriminated, exploited in the distant lands by the dadan subcontracts.

The terms of contract between contractor and subcontractor and between subcontractor and labourer are oral. Even when a small house owner recruits labour directly from market place, only oral contract exists.

Thus, the system of subcontract and temporary nature of work, have resulted in the recruitment of thousands of construction labourers on subcontract and casual basis. There are the principal employers with massive capital outlay at one end of the complex chain of hierarchical relationships and lakhs of construction workers with highly insecure subsistence living standards on the other end. In between lies a whole hierarchy of intermediaries, contractors and subcontractors so that there is no link between employer and labourers. The invisibility of the labourers, and specifically, of the women labour has left the women to work in this industry with terms of employment, type of work, housing and living conditions determined by the nature of recruitment.

Types of Recruitment

Since contracting, subcontracting and labour contract were the methods by which construction was carried out in the public and private sectors, there was no difference with regard to recruitment modes between public and private sectors. But the recruitment of labour differed according to size of construction, big medium or small.

There are broadly three types of recruitment:

(i) Workers directly recruited by contractor and housed in the site;

(ii) Workers recruited from rural areas by subcontractors or labour contractors on certain norms and conditions by advancing loans known as dadan labourers;

(iii) Workers recruited from City Slums or pavements market places by principal employers or maistris.

In the big construction sites the first and second types of recruitment were the most prevalent. There were women recruited by contractors retained on master roll for long number of years but kept as temporary hands. They were housed on sites and kept moving from they need more hands at works for a few days, depend on the market place labour.

Objectives of the Study

(i) The study aims at analysing the history, organisation nature and working of construction sector in our country.

(ii) The study examines the socio-economic conditions of informal women construction labourers with special reference to Ganjam district of Orissa.

Methodology

Keeping the objective in view it was decided to collect data from construction site from women labourers during their off time. Data relating to socio-economic variable like terms and conditions of work, nature of work, wage rate, wage discrimination, provision of health care, security measures etc. have been collected with the help of a questionnaire.

The data so collected with the help of questionnaire, interviews, observations and field notes by visiting several rounds to the sites have been for the purpose of analysis.

Relations and Terms of Employment in According to Size of Construction

There is no direct employer-employee relation for most of the labourers. Only the directly recruited labourers of contractors employed by house owners for small repair works, had a direct relationship with their employers.

In small repair works this relationship continues for a few days a week. In such cases number of workers are meager. In general however, most of the labourers are recruited by labour subcontractors and labourers have no direct relation with employers. Since the maistries recruited the labour, supervised the work and made wage payments, the labourers consider them to be the actual employers. Thus, not only is the labour invisible to the employers but the employers are also invisible to labourers since subcontractors determine the conditions of employment according to the convenience of the contractors.

Nature of Works Performed by Women Labourers

In earth work, the men dig the foundation holes and fill the baskets with mud using spades, while women carry the earth deposit them in the place allotted for it. Even though normally digging is done by male hands, it is not uncommon to find women handling crowbar and spade in earth work.

Masonry work involves construction of walls with brick and mortar and smoothing the surface of the walls, floor and roof as soon as the cement is applied while both men and women prepare the mortar, women carry the bricks, mortar and water to place the mason is at work. She also assists mason in his work.

Curing work is mostly undertaken by women. As soon as concreting is over, the floors, roofs and walls have to be continuously wet with water. The water is allowed to stand on the floor in order that the mortar and cement would settle and dry properly. Curing has to be continued for a period of 10 days.

Breaking Jalli in done by women. The bricks have to be broken into small pieces using a hammer, for laying the floor.

Concreting work involves both men and women. The materials required for concrete mixture is usually assembled near the machine by men, if this involves carrying bags of cement or sand. After the mixture is made , men and women from a human chain all along the scaffolding until the spot where jalli has to be deposited. In quick succession the bondli full of mixture is passed from one hand to another, and the work goes on the whole day as jalli work has to be completed within a single day.

In big sites more women are employed to do only concreting work while in small sites most women do combination of all types of works like carrying cement, water, sand, brick etc.

Quantum of Work

An attempt has been at estimating the quantum and intensity of work done by female workers in certain areas of construction work. We tried to measure it in a period of five minutes for different types of work done by women, namely, masonry, concreting, curing and earth work.

In concreting where the bondlies of concrete mixture is passed from one hand to another, it was found that 40 bondlies passed through the hands of a women in 10 minutes.

For masonry work, the women was found carrying 10 to 12 wet bricks on her head and sometimes climbing the scaffolding with the load on her head with great skill and grace. Each wet brick weighed about 2 Kg.

In curing she was found carrying water in a pot 10 times in an hour and pouring the water each time over the concrete structures. Each pot weighed 7 kgs.

As everywhere else in the construction work too there exists division of work between men and women in the unskilled jobs. All tough jobs such as balancing 12 bricks on the head while climbing the ladder and passing the bondlies of mixture along the heights in quick succession, require dexterity and skill along with great stamina and yet they are termed "unskilled " jobs by everyone concerned. In this division of labour that had been described above, men and women are paid differently by the sub-contractor. Wherever division of labour exists, no matter what work women do, the value of the work is considered less than that of a male labourer. This wage differentials become even more glaring where they do the same job such as concreting, and still get paid less than their male counterparts. Notwithstanding the fact that women do all the various types of work in many instances, women are always considered to be the lowest in the hierarchy of the system of subcontract and therefore paid the lowest in construction work.

Wage Rates and Number of Days of Work

The wage rates are lowest for women labour in all construction sites. The wage rates bore an inverse relation to regularity of employment and thus, to the size of construction in Berhampur city. The daily wage rates of women varied from Rs. 30 to Rs. 40. In the big sites the workers were paid the least while they were assured of continuous employment for 20-22 days a month. In the small sector the market place women were paid the minimum of Rs. 30 but the number of days of employment was less than 14. In the big constructions including the public sector sites, minimum wages were violated with impunity. Work experience is not taken into account in fixing wage rates. Thus, a women with long years of experience is paid the same wage as a novice. Interviews among women labourers revealed the aforesaid facts.

Wage Differential Between Men and Women

In masonry the work done by men and women were similar but had difference. The men would bring cement bags, prepare the mix and put it in the bondli. The women carries bricks, stones, cement, mortar and supply them for use in the construction works. While at an average male labourers receive Rs. 45 per day in private works, females receive only Rs. 35. In the event of accidents, sickness or during maternity, workers had to forgo employment and wages. They got indebted during these periods either to moneylenders or neighbours (in small sites and market places) or to subcontractors (in big sites and among maistri attached labour). Mostly the rural labourers of Gangam and Puri are indebted to labour contractors. Such labourers are known as dadan labourers who employed outside the state and exploited by labour contractors.[5]

Mode of Payment

Usually, the subcontractors and maistris received payment in piece-rate while labourers were paid on day rate. As the maistries were responsible for recruitment of workers, supervision and disbursement of wages, they were able to secure more money by inflating on record the number of workers under them in case of public sector undertaking constructions.

Facilities

The construction labourers are provided with practically no amenities not even the basic amenities such as wholesome drinking water, toilets and urinals. Provision of these as well as canteens restrooms and creches are mandatory according to Contract Labour Regulation Act. The Act states that if contractor fails to provide amenities, the principal employer can provide them and recover the cost from the contractor. But in construction sites all these were conspicuously absent. Lack of toilets on the sites put women to a great deal of inconvenience.

Health Care

The women often complained of neck pain, chest pain, headache, body ache and fever exhaustion and problems arising out of carrying wet construction materials on their heads. In big sites where there was continuous employment, they were compelled to rest for a few days every fortnight to recoup their energies. In general, no medical facility was provided by the employers and the labourers were compelled to spend money for medical care. Visit to hospitals meant that the labourers had to forgo their works as well as wages for the day.

Maternity and Child Care

Women do heavy manual work even till the day of delivery. About 40% of the children born to these construction women were delivered by neighbouring women or relatives or by traditional midwives. During the first delivery most women stayed at home up to one year before returning to work. From the next, delivery on wards they stayed for a period ranging from one month to three months.

Again because the industry did not compensate the women for loss of her earnings, she becomes indebted either to subcontractors or to money lenders. In big sites it was found that when a women was to deliver, the husband too stayed away from work in order to look after the wife. As they has to take loans form the subcontractors they were compelled to join work at the earliest with a view to repaying of loan.

In our analysis, 30 per cent of the women carried the children to the work site, 20% left them on their own at home, 25% left the infants in the care of elder girls or persons, 15% are sent to schools, 10% are employed in shops and commercial establishments.

Children on the site were exposed to the health hazards children were grossly neglected in the work site. Some times they quarrel themselves and sometimes play among themselves. Children were seen playing in the cement water, sands etc. Thus the total lack of child care facility seemed to affect the lives of the children of women labour in this sector.

Occupational Hazards and Accidents

The risk involved in construction work is very high particularly for women workers, who have to climb great heights carrying heavy loads. Accidents involving simple injuries occur every day while fatal accidents are not uncommon. Falling from heights, electric shock, falling of objects, and collapse of ladder, are the major reasons for fatal accidents, as revealed from interviews and field notes.

Long hours of work involving continuous handling of cement, lime or other corrosive construction materials lead to the feet and hands being bruised burnt and eaten away. Women workers who carry the cement mix and wet bricks on their heads suffer serious problems like headache and fever. Pregnant women who carry heavy loads run a high risk of abortion.

There are no rules for safety in construction. Most of the women labourers have belonged to the landless agricultural labourers and migrants. Women labourers mainly from Lochapada, Bhabinipur, Khodasing , Lanjipalli have revealed that they visit to their work in little family groups. After their return, they have to prepare food for the family members. Thus, women labourers are doubly exploited and overburdened.

Socio-Economic Profile of Informal Women Labour

Size of the Family

Size of the family counts to the members present in the family. Normally, the family comprising less than five members is considered as a small family and above that a large family. Table—14 depicts the clear picture of the size of family of the 50 informal women labour in the construction sector.

Table—14
Size of the family in the informal women labourers in construction sector

S.No.	*Size of the family*	*Frequency*	*Per centage (Approximate)*
1	0-2	4	8.0
2	3-5	20	40.0
3	6-8	21	42.0
4	9-11	5	10.0
Total		**50**	**100**

Source: Field Studies

The foregoing table reveals that only 48 per cent of construction women labourers belong to small families having a size of 1 to 5 members, 42 per cent belong to large families with 6 to 8 members. The rest 10 per cent of women construction workers belong to very large family of 9 to 11 members.

The Caste Structure

In India the caste structure shows the socio-economic status of the people. It also determines the socio-political consciousness of the people. The barriers between high and low castes creates obstacles in the path of economic growth by restricting social mobility of labour force and creating contract among higher castes for manual works. In the present study the caste structure has been divided into three groups: (I) General Caste, (II) The Scheduled Castes (SC), (III) Scheduled Tribes (ST)

Table—15
Caste Structure of the Woman Households

Caste	*No of Respondents*	*Percentage*
General Caste (GC)	28	56
Scheduled Caste (SC)	17	34
Scheduled Tribe (ST)	05	10
Total	**50**	**100**

Source: Field Studies

An analysis of the Table—15 reveals that 56 per cent of the women construction households belong to the General Caste, 34 per cent of the total workers belong to the Scheduled Caste and 10 per cent belong to the Scheduled Tribes.

It has been confirmed from the sample data that all the Scheduled Tribe Workers have migrated to Berhampur from other places like Phulbani and Ganjapati District. These informal women labourers in slums around Braza Nagar of Berhampur city. The other migrated construction women labourers belong to rural areas of the district.

Educational Composition of the Sample Households

Education is a good index for human resource development. Investment on education is more powerful instrument for the socio-economic and cultural transformation of the people.

Illiteracy causes ignorance which is responsible for the narrow socio-economic attitude of the people. Narrowness of the social and economic attitude of people hampers their productive capacity and automatically keeps them away from the formal or organised sectors.

Some idea regarding the literacy position among the women labourers in the construction work of Berhampur city is revealed from the Table—16.

Table—16
Educational Composition of Women Construction Labourers

Educational Level	*No. of Labourers*	*Percentage*
1. Nil	27	54
2. Lower Primary	12	24
3. Upper Primary	08	16
4. M.E. School	03	06
5. Matriculation and above	Nil	Nil
Total	**50**	**100**

Source: Data Collected and Compiled

It is found from Table—16 that 54 per cent of the women construction labourers in the study are illiterate. They were not admitted to any school at all. As many as 46 per cent of the women workers were admitted to the school out of which 24 per cent were at the lower primary level 16 per cent were at the upper primary level and only a meager percentage of 6 were at middle school level.

Housing Conditions of the Sample Households

Ideal housing conditions generally promote the state of health and efficiency of the workers. Lack of housing facility and inferior housing accommodation is the indicator of backwardness and poverty. Obviously, good housing facility is necessary for workers to make them efficient and committed to work.

In the present study all the respondents are living in thatched houses and cottages made of straw and clay. The rooms are very small in size. The number of rooms available in each thatched house is also not adequate.

Table—17 shows the accommodation (number of rooms) available in the houses of informal women construction labourers under study.

Table—17
Number of Rooms in the Houses of Sample Construction Labourers

No of Rooms	*Frequency*	*Per centage*
One room	26	52
Two rooms	18	36
Three rooms	06	12
More than 3 rooms	Nil	Nil
Total	**50**	**100**

Source: Field Studies

About 52 per cent of the labourers in our analysis are living in single room and 36 per cent of the families in homes with two rooms. The rest 12 per cent of the households possessed only 3 rooms. None of the families was living in houses with more than 3 rooms, as revealed from the Table—17.

All the family members of the construction women labourers live in the same room without any ventilation, which results in poor hygienic conditions of the labourers. None of the house is electrified. All respondents are using tap water supplied by the municipality at different parts of the street. No latrine facility is available to the houses of the respondents. The floors remain swampy during rainy season.

Habit of the Informal Women Labourers

Habit determine the size of expenditure and the mental physical health of the labourers. It is revealed from the Table—18 that 50 per cent of the respondents among the sample households are accustomed to some habits. The data presented in the table further reveal the kind of habits the households have, and the daily average expenditure of each worker on respective habits.

Table—18
Percentage Distribution of the Main Habits and the Average Daily Expenditure of Sample Households

S.No.	*Kind of main habit*	*No. of women labourers*	*Percentage of women labourers*	*Daily average expenditure of women labourers in respective habits (in ruppes)*
1	Drinking	05	10	10
2	Taking Tamakhu	08	16	04
3	Chewing betel	15	30	04
4	Taking tea and coffee	16	32	06
5	Visiting cinema	05	10	10
6	Other habits	01	02	05
	Total	**50**	**100**	

Source: Field Studies

Table—18 clearly shows that 32 per cent of the labourers are accustomed to tea and coffee and each labourer has to spend a minimum of Rs. 6 daily towards the same. About 30 per cent of the labourers are accustomed to chewing betel and every one spends Rs. 4 per day on this. Again, 16 per cent of the labourers are accustomed to taking Tamakhu (gudakhu) and each has to spend Rs. 4 daily on this habit.

Table—19
Percentage Distribution of Sources of Information about the Construction Work

Various Sources		*No of Households*	*Percentage*
1.	Parents	04	08
2.	Relatives	10	20
3.	Mediators	28	56
4.	Unknown Persons	06	12
5.	Self	02	04
	Total	**50**	**100**

Source : Field Studies

It is found from the Table—19 that 56 per cent of the informal women labourers get employment information from the mediators like mistries and contractors, and 20 per cent get information from their relatives.

Each of the remaining sources of information such as parents, unknown persons, self and other cover 24 per cent of the sample informal women labour households.

Nature of Works

The study reveals that the informal women labourers are engaged in carrying a heavy weight of chips, bricks, water, timber, cement etc. to the work place.

It is found through interrogation that 46 per cent of the women labourers are engaged in carrying sand chips and bricks to the work spot, 30 per cent of them are engaged in preparing concrete and the rest 24 per cent are engaged in providing concrete to the mistries.

The Economic Background of Sample Households

Under the economic background of the informal women construction labour, working hours, leave facilities, leisure in between the working hours, distance of work place to their villages, conveyances availed to reach the work spot, social relationship with their employers, awareness of women labour about their exploitation, indebtedness, form of property owned, duration of employment, morbidity, attitude, beliefs etc. have been presented.

Payment of wages to the Informal Women Labour

Almost all the sample workers accept jobs to earn wage to supplement to the family income. They accept the prevailing wage usually offered by the mistries. The urban wage is higher that the wage in rural areas. In our sample, more that 60 per cent of the migrants joined in their jobs shortly after migration to the city at the prevailing wage rate.

The system of wage payment in the construction industry is not uniform. Minimum wages fixed for certain unskilled work categories vary from state to state. In Orissa, minimum daily wage has been fixed at 40 rupees since a decade back which has not been revised. It is found that the women labourers are paid less than the male workers, and the prevailing wage is higher that the minimum wages in urgent cases as the latter has not been revised.

Even different wages are given to different groups of women workers employed in the same town and even in the same work site. The skilled mistries get wage at the piece rate but an unskilled women worker is given wage at the time-rate. In case of high demand for a construction work, the women labourers paid little more than the prevailing daily wage.

The National Commission on Labour (1969) has therefore Rightly Pointed out

"The system of wage payment by contractors to sub-contractors on piece rate basis and of the payment by the latter to individual workers and daily rates is subject to abuse "Report of the National Commission of Labour"—Government of India 1969. (Publication Division).

Informal women workers sometimes report about non-payment, short-measurement of the works by the mistries and other intermediaries. In this regard they are no free from exploitation. Again the women labourers in the informal sector are paid less than their counterparts in the formal construction sector.

Dr. Samal in his study of urban informal sector of Sambalpur district of Orissa remarks:

"The difference in earnings between formal and informal sectors are no doubt significant but not in fact very large and less than among the different segments of the informal sector itself"[6]

Table—20
Daily Wage Distribution of Sample Women Labourers in Construction Sector

Wages(in Rs.)	*Frequency*	*Percentage*
30	26	52
35	15	30
40	09	18
Total	**50**	**100**

Source: Field Studies

Table—20 reveals that 52 per cent of the female workers are paid wages of Rs.30 per day, 30 per cent of the female are paid Rs. 35/- and 18 per cent women labourers received wage of Rs.40/- per day.

Table—21
Percentage Distribution Showing Indebtendness and Reasons for Incurring Debts by Sample Labourers

Reasons for Incurring Debt	*Frequency*	*Percentage of Workers*
1. Daily expenditure	26	52
2. Marriage	12	24
3. Illness	08	16
4. Purchasing Cart/Bullock etc.	04	08
Other Purpose	*Nil*	*Nil*
Total	**50**	**100**

Source: Field Studies

At the time of study, some of the respondents has little savings in the banks and post offices. They did not reach the banks for loans as they did not have any idea about the banking procedures for taking such loans nor also have time to spare.

The women workers used to take loans from the village landlords and contractors which were to be repaid in the earliest opportunity. It is revealed from the Table—21 that almost 60 per cent of the respondents were in debt at the time of study. About 69 per cent of the borrowers had taken loans in order to meet the marriage expenses and illness in the family. Only 24 per cent found it necessary to take loans in order meet their normal daily expenditure. Because inadequate earning and increased consumption the respondents had to take the loans from the village moneylenders, relatives, mistries and contractors.

Form of Assets Owned by the Respondents and Monthly Income of Labourers under Study

In India poverty is caused due to the lack of income generating assets. Because of nonpossession of such assets, the unskilled poor women labour depend on physical labour only.

Physical labour yields inadequate income and thereby keeps them in the vicious circle of poverty. Low and irregular income cause misery to the poverty-stricken women labour households.

As revealed from Table—22 almost 32 per cent of the respondents have their residential houses. Only 20 per cent of the respondents own some cultivable land, 48 per cent of the respondents are residing in the rented house.

Table—22
Percentage Distribution of Assets Owned by the Respondents

Form of Asset	*Frequency*	*Percentage*
Agricultural Land	10	20
House (Residential)	16	32
Rented house	24	48
Total	50	**100**

Source: Field Studies

A perusal of the study brings into light that the unskilled labour is largely concentrated in constructed sector of urban centres. This labour force is partly drawn from the city and largely from the adjoining villages of the cities and towns. The work is seasonal and casual. Women labour is usually preferred to carry on the construction work. There is rapid expansion of the construction work in the urban centres and unskilled labour force among the women who have been attracted towards this sector.

The employment of women in the urban construction sector in not direct. They work under the direct control of the mistri and the contractors. There is a frequent change of work place and hence women move from place to place to carry on the construction work. They are asked to work for longer hours and paid lower wages. The question of job security in this sector does not arise. The construction workers are unorganised.

Majority of women workers prefer to work under a known contractor or mistri. They cover a long distance to reach the work place. In addition to the construction work they perform unpaid works for the contractors and mistries and do all household works at home. Socially and economically backward, such workers don't have any future plan. They prefer to work in groups. The seasonal nature of the work causes misery to them during rainy seasons.

The problems and difficulties of working women in the construction industry are multi-dimensional. The socio-economic and psycho-environmental problems and difficulties are faced by these working women both at home and at work. The problems faced by them can be summarised in the following words:

(i) It is observed that the largeness of the family is the most important cause that breeds poverty and compels them to accept a job whatever the wage may be;

(ii) The study reveals that 54 per cent of gross illiteracy among the large mass of working women is responsible for their immobility, exploitation, misery and poverty. Poor economic conditions of the parents, distance of educational institutions from their respective villages and their age old engagement in agricultural lands as well as in the construction works are some of the factors which stands as obstacles in the continuation of their study;

(iii) About 52 per cent family members of the women construction labourers live in small rooms without any ventilation. The thatched cottages are subjected to fire. During the rainy season they witness untold misery as the ghostly winds washout the straw around them. These cause a chronic problem to the dwellers and the belonging of the house as well;

(iv) The monthly earning of women in the informal sector is much less than the earning in the formal sector. Even the wages paid to labourers in different urban informal sub-sectors vary to a great extent;

(v) The majority of migrant informal sector women labourers are found to be in debt, but despite abject poverty, the indebtedness among the native workers is not significant;

(vi) The informal women labourers work for longer hours;

(vii) A large majority of informal women labourers are habituated to tea, betels, tomakhu etc. These habits unknowingly take 10 to 15 per cent of their daily income. The same amount is also spent on non-working days;

(viii) The women labourers are exploited at work place and at home. They are unaware of being exploited. Lack of unionisation, gross illiteracy and grinding poverty among the working women have the way for exploitation.

Almost all the relevant protective labour laws are applicable to the construction workers covered under the study. Such laws include the Factories Act 1948, Workmen's Compensation Act 1923, The Maternity Benefits Act 1961, The Contract Labour Regulation and Abolition Act 1970, Equal Remuneration Act 1976 etc. The State Governments have also drafted regulations for controlling the terms and conditions of employment of labour in the unorganised sectors. The contractors are under the legal obligation to follow these regulations and provide facilities and amenities to their workers including the women workers. But it appears that in majority of these regulations are violated by the employers. Though the study did not attempt to know the reasons for non-implementation of these regulations, it is not difficult to form the impression that no serious attempt has been made by the Government to see that these regulations are enforced.

The enforcement of the laws and regulations drafted by the Union and State Governments would be a great way towards alleviating the living and working conditions of labourers particularly the informal women labourers employed in the urban unorganised construction sector.

SECTION—B

Informal Women Labour in Domestic Households

An attempt has been made to highlight the general social and economic characteristics of 50 domestic household labourers selected at random from the city of Berhampur. The socio-economic features cover the caste structure, the marital status, the size of the family, the literacy position of the sample units, the asset position, monthly income of the units under study, period of stay in the city, nature of work, the working conditions etc.

A woman employed in domestic households is called a 'kamabali' or 'maid-servant'. Such women broadly be divided into two categories on the basis of their nature of employment. Some of them are part-timers and others are full-timers. 'The part-time women labourers serve in more than one family and in each house work for a specific period only. The other informal women labourers serve in only one family and carry the work-load for the whole day. Again the second category of labourers can be divided into two on the basis of the condition of their employment. Some women labourers stay in the families in which they are employed and the other women labourers work in the family for a wage and do not remain there. They usually return to their own houses after the completion of the household work in the employer's family.

In urban areas usually a middle class family employs a woman labourer to assist the housewife in the household work. To some extent employment of a woman is a necessity to the family where the housewife is also an employee. In such cases the housewife is bound to employ a woman to assist in her domestic household works.

The present study makes an humble attempt to highlight the socio-economic and psychological aspects of the problems of such informal women labour employed in domestic households of Berhampur city.

Since this section is devoted to highlighting the socio-economic problems of domestic household workers, a list of works that women perform in domestic households for which they are paid has been presented. This includes the works done essentially outside the household to pursue one's own independent profession. The other category includes all the household works that the women perform in their own families for which they are not paid.

Table—23
'Paid Works' and 'Unpaid Works' of Women in India

Category of work	*Items of Activities*
1. Paid Work (Work done in other households for wage)	*(a)* Sweeping, cleaning of residential house and its surroundings.
	(b) Washing clothing and utensils of household.
	(c) Cooking (including grinding of grain, pulses, cutting of vegetables, fruits, etc.) for household members and guests.
	(d) Child care.
	(e) Attending to old, disabled and diseased members of household.
	(f) Fetching drinking water for household use.
	(g) Collecting fuel and firewood for household use.
	(h) Purchases of groceries, garments and household necessities.
	(i) Sewing and mending of clothing for household use.
	(j) Tatoring of household children.
	(k) Observance of social and religious duties.

(Contd . . .)

2. Unpaid work (Work done in own household)	
	(a) Preparation of rice, flour etc. from paddy, wheat and other cereals.
	(b) Pounding of rice, pulses, spices etc.
	(c) Milking of cows for production milk for household consumption.
	(d) Attending to household cattle.
	(e) Preparation of ghee, butter curd etc. exclusively for household consumption.
	(f) Papad, achar, sauce, pickle making for household consumption.
	(g) Attending to household poultry for production of eggs exclusively for household consumption.
	(h) Manufacture of chira, muri and similar other products from rice, other cereals, pulses etc.
	(i) Helping male members of household in minor construction, repair of own house and cattle sheds, thatching of roof, construction of fencing, etc.

Source: Field Studies.

Marital Status of the Women Workers

In a male dominated society, the status of women is determined by the status of men in the family. A married woman's status is determined by the status of her husband. The women work for a wage with a view to supplementing to the family income. The misery of the women starts when the husband, the earning member of the family, looses his ability to work and earn bread for the family. This is true to most of the women workers under study.

Table—24
Marital Status of Sample Households

	Marital Status	*Frequency*	*Percentage*
1.	Living with husband	34	64
2.	Divorced	4	8
3.	Widows	10	20
4.	Unmarried	2	4
	Total	**50**	**100**

Source: Field Studies

The Table—24 reveals the marital status of 50 sample women workers. As many as 48 out of samples women workers got married below 20 years of age. Excepting two woman labourers the rest are married. Out of 48 married women 10 are widows, 4 are divorcees and the rest 34 are living with their husbands.

It is found that 20 per cent of the women have been forced to work outside due to the death of the main earning member. Twenty eight per cent the sample units are divorcees and widows. Inadequate earning of the male member forces the women labourers to engage themselves as domestic servants and go out-side to work as has been found in case of 34 households out of 50 sample households. Next to this, the factors like death, divorce or separation brings untold misery to the family and results in women to work outside for a wage. Usually the married women are preferred to work in domestic households as they are experienced in household article being misused.

Caste Distribution of the Sample Workers

It has been told earlier that customs and traditions about sexual division of labour place women in an unfavourable situation. Caste system restricts social and geographical mobility of labour in India. Hence, it is necessary to know about the caste distribution of the sample units.

Table—25
Caste distribution of the Sample Labourers

	Caste Group	*No. of workers*	*Percentage*
1.	Brahmin	24	48
2.	Non-Brahmin	25	50
3.	Scheduled Tribe	01	02
	Total	50	**100**

Source: Field Studies

Table—25 depicts the caste distribution of the sample units. Out of 50 sample workers, 24 are Brahmins; (48 per cent), 25 are non-Brahmins (50 per cent) and (2 per cent) belong to the Scheduled Tribes. The study also reveals both Hindus and non-Hindus participate in the domestic household labour. While appointing maid servants the households usually prefer women of the same caste. Almost all Hindu families give priority to Brahmin women. The non-Brahmin women working in Brahmin families are not allowed to enter the kitchen and other sacred places. Since the upper middle caste belongs to the general caste group, women of lower castes (Scheduled Tribe) are not preferred to work as domestic servants even in urban educated families. This implies that even today caste feeling has not yet disappeared from the minds of the urban educated elite.

Age Composition of Sample Workers

In a developing country like India, women and children participate in the labour force at an early age with a view to supplementing to the family income. Child labour is seen everywhere in India and elsewhere in the third world. Table—26 reveals the age composition of the sample units.

Table—26
Age Composition of Sample Labourers

Age Group (in year)	*Frequency*	*Percentage of works*
Below 20	02	04
21-30	12	24
31-40	16	32
41-50	14	28
Above 50	06	12
Total	50	**100**

Source : Field Data

Table—26 reveals that women belonging to different age groups participate in a domestic household service sector. Two unmarried women below 20 years are found among the sample household in our study. This middle-aged women workers are preferred to work as they are considered to be more capable and experienced. Again these women are considered suitable to perform strenuous household works. There are 12 women belonging to the age group of 21-30 years. 16 women of 31-40 years. 14 women of 41-50 years and 6 women are having an age of more than 50 years.

Literacy Position of Women

The generation of skill and knowledge for the labour force is a somewhat more tangible function of education. Hence education is an important determinant of ability to work and earn. According to the census report of 1991, almost 60 per cent women in India are illiterate. Lack of education compels them to join in the low paid informal sectors like agriculture, construction and allied domestic household services, where, they are paid low wages. On the other hand, in developed countries majority of women labourers are educated and hence skilled. They join in formal sectors where they earn more and avail all the facilities afforded by the formal sector.

Table—27
The Educational Composition of the Women Labourers

	Level of Education	*Frequency*	*Percentage*
1.	Nil	38	76
2.	Upto Class—III	08	16
3.	Upto M.E. School	04	08
4.	Upto H.S.C.	Nil	Nil
	Total	**50**	**100**

Source: Field Studies

It is depicted from the Table—27 that out of 50 sample, as many as 38 women are illiterate. Only 12 are literate. It can be concluded form the data that illiteracy is a predominant characteristic of the women labour households and is the cause of their poverty. Pitiable economic condition and lack of interest in the education of girl-child can be the cause of the existing magnitude of illiteracy among working women.

Conditions of Residential House of the Sample Workers

Most of the sample women labourers live in small houses with not more than two rooms. Only 40 per cent of the houses of the workers are having temporary latrines and no house is supplied with tap water. The water supplied by the municipality is used as drinking water. Some women labour household live as which have temporary connections from the neighbouring house owners.

Size of the Family of the Women Domestic Workers

The size of the family and the age composition of the members of the family determine the standard of living. The larger the size of the family, the greater is its economic burden.

Table—28
Size of the Family of the Women Domestic Labourers

Size of the Family	*Frequency*	*Percentage*
1-2	4	8
3-4	10	20
5-6	27	54
7-8	9	18
Above 8	Nil	Nil
Total	**50**	**100**

Source: Field Studies

Table—28 depicts that out of the size of the family of 50 women households under study, only 4 women households are having 2 members, 10 households are having members between 3-4, 27 workers are having 5-6 members and workers are having 7-8 members. No worker is living in a family with more than 8 members. As many as 72 per cent of women workers belong to the families with more than 4 members. Larger family can be the cause of poverty of much informal women labour which compels them to enter into the profession.

Women Workers Under Study

It has been said earlier that migration to the cities in third worked countries is mainly due to the economic backwardness of the rural areas. In India the rural labour force is pushed away to the cities under similar circumstances. The unskilled and semiskilled rural labour force finds inadequate revenue of employment opportunity in the rural areas and therefore, migrates to the urban areas in search of employment opportunities. Finding restricted employment opportunity in the formal sector, they are compelled to accept low paid urban informal sub-sectors like construction works, domestic households and household industries. Out of 50 women workers under study 38 are migrants and only 12 are the permanent residents of the city. All these 38 migrants have migrated to the city with their family members. Despite several efforts made to uplift the rural poor through various scheme like DWCRA, ICDS, JRY, etc, the migration to the urban areas has continued unabated.

Table—29 depicts the causes of migration and the period of stay in the city by such migrant informal women labourers.

Table—29
Percentage distribution showing the period of stay in the city

Length of the period of stay in yrs.	*Number of Sample Households*	*Percentage*
Upto 2 years	14	28
Above 2 upto 4 years	16	32
Above 4 upto 6 years	08	08
Above 10 years	12 (permanent residents)	24
Total	50	**100**

Source: Field Studies.

It is seen that 14 out of 38 migrants resided in the city for a period of 2 years, 16 women labourers have stayed for a period between 2-4 years 18 labourers between 4-6. Only 12 are the permanent residents of the city. All the sample women labourers who have migrated to the city in search of jobs either along with the make members or following the migration of the other members of the family.

Average Monthly Income of the Family Members

The urban informal sector provides job opportunities to the unskilled migrants by offering them lower wages. Hence income earned by these workers is not high. The pattern of monthly earnings of the families of the household workers has seen analysed in the Table—30.

Table—30
The Family Income Distribution of Women Labourers

Monthly Income in Rs	*Number of Families*	*Percentage*
Rs. 201-400	Nil	Nil
Rs. 401-600	15	30
Rs. 601-800	25	50
Above 800	10	20
Total	**50**	**100**

Source: Field Studies

Table—30 reveals that no family earns an income of less than Rs. 400 per month; 15 families earn an income between Rs. 401 and 600 per month 25 families earn an income of Rs. 601 and 800 (50 per cent) and 10 families (20 per cent) is having an average monthly income of more than 800 rupees. Wage income constitute the major source of income for all the sample households.

Cause of Migration to the City

Almost all the migrant women labourer households who the city consequent upon the migration of the husband and other family members. Out of 50 sample units 38 migrant women workers (12 being the permanent residents) have migrated to the city because of poverty or other reasons. Rural indebtedness and unemployment are the cause of the rural push of such migrants as stated by the sample internal women labourers (more than 47 per cent)

Table—31
Percentage Distribution of Women Labour Regarding the Cause of Migration

Cause of Migration	*Number of families*	*Percentage of families*
1. Poverty in native place	15	39.47
2. Search of employment	18	47.37
3. Other causes	5	13.16
Total	38	**100.00**

Source: Field Studies

Attitude of Women Workers towards Female Education, Equal Wage Payment to Women and Family Planning.

The Social and economic condition determine the attitude of an individual. Efforts have been made to know the attitude of such sample labourers towards female education, equal wage for equal work by men and women and need for family planning.

Out of 50 sample units 43 are of the opinion that girls should be given education just sufficient for reading and writing. The rest 7 workers were in favour of higher education to be given to girls. The former group believes that highly educated women will prefer highly educated men and hence, there may be a problem of dowry.

It is interesting to note that 42 sample women are not in favour of giving equal wage to men and women. They opinion that men are more capable and hence deserve higher wages even for the same work. Only 8 sample, women labourers argued in favour of equalisation of wages for men and women. Out of 50 sample workers 48 were married. They were in favour of adopting family planning norms. But 12 women are apprehensive about the safety of family divices. Some of them are on notion that adoption of family planning devices reduced the working capacity of men and women.

Construction vis-a-vis Domestic Household Workers

Construction and domestic households are the two important informal urban subsectors providing employment to a large majority of women unskilled workers. Though in these in these two sub-sectors women labour is subject to exploitation from the point of view of low wages being paid to the, longer working hours and denial of leave and leisure, some differences between the two sub-sectors are worth mentioning here.

The construction work is purely seasonal in nature. The labour is causal. The labour in this sector is drawn from surrounding areas of the city. Hardly 15 per cent of the construction labour is drawn from the city. Such workers are more migratory in nature. There is frequent change of work site and a woman worker is exposed to sun and dust. The job involves greater risk. Such women workers are more adoptive. Only young and able bodied women are demanded for such works. The wage is paid almost daily. Both men and women work under the same mistri and the women are paid less than men in this sector. On the other hand, domestic household sector imposes a caste bar. The women belonging to upper castes find better chances of employment in this sector. The work is not seasonal. The women perform a number of household works. They are mainly drawn from the temporarily settled rural-pushed labour force who are paid monthly. The work involves less risk. In addition to their wage these women enjoy some fringe benefits. Their job is purely temporary. Domestic informal women servants enjoy little more leave and leisure than the construction workers. The work in the household sector is not as hard as in the case of construction works. These labourer maintain closer contact with the employer.

The women construction workers get higher wage than the domestic maid servants. In the case of household sector, an urban employer prefers to employ a local caste woman. Hence, such works are not available for the migrated low caste women. The domestic servants consider the work of muliani as inferior with the growth of a middle class, the demand for domestic servants is increasing. The construction work is flourishing in most of the urban centers of our country. Hence these two sectors are absorbing a sizeable portion of the unskilled women labour force. Absence of unionisation and casual nature of the construction work are the two most important causes of exploitation of women labour. Of the two, the construction worker is subject to greater exploitation. The construction mistri making contacts charges to the owner at the piece-rate, but the wage is paid to the labourer at the time rate. The longer the working hour, the higher is rate of profit and hence the greater is the exploitation of construction workers.

Conclusion

The study reveals that women make no less contribution to the national income than that of the men folk. Women in addition to their paid work, perform a number of economic activities outside the house. Their contribution is not properly assessed by men in a male dominated society. As the National

Commission (1987) has rightly observed "Women's Contribution to the family and the National economy remains largely invisible and undervalue." Her potentialities are not fully realised due to the structural constraints as involved and institutionalised by men.

In India deprivation of women is more acute in terms of health, education, nutrition, social, economic, political and demographic aspects. Under pressure and forces of traditional, cultural as well as historical factors women have been ignored rather denied opportunities for participating in the process of development and sharing its benefits. Unfortunately, her great asset of reproduction to perpetuates human race has become her great handicap. Leaving asides her claim to equality and non discriminatory treatment it is intended that women are born for marriage. They are deprived of any material or non-material reward. Her rewards lie in servitude, silent suffering and performance of her duty within the four walls in the households. Reason for her suffering in that she herself is not conscious of the rọle she performs as house maker and as an economic contributor to the family income.

Even the urban woman labourers are equally self-effacing and lack in urge for self development. She believes that men and women are meant for different roles in which man is superior.

The study clearly reveals that women prefer to work outside to maintain the livelihood. Indeed a working woman enjoys a better status in the family than a non-working house wife. But a change in the material status of the working woman does not add to her physical and mental condition mainly due to the strain she has to sustain while carrying on the unpaid household work and the paid work outside her home. Out of all the services in India domestic labour is the most unregulated and disorganized. There are no written contracts or protective regulations. The highly personalised nature of the work further complicates the situation. In 1987 Sarvekshana reported that 1.68 million female workers are toiling in the domestic sector as opposed to 0.68 male workers.

It has been observed that because of iniquitous social structure and gender bias in the performance of domestic chores including child rearing, informal women labourers are doubly exploited. It is also observed that in addition to spending around 10 hours (including the time spent to attend the work site) at the place of work, a woman labourer devotes 4 hours on the domestic chores. Thus, the informal women labourers are over-burdened due to their engagements in wage earning. Some of the informal women labourers have reported that the attitude and behaviours of female labourers are not encouraging. It is revealed from the informal discussion with the construction women labourers that the employer contractor sometimes abuse them which the latter do not expose for fear of social sanction.

The informal women labourers both in the construction and domestic service sectors are substantially subjugated to the tradition bound status at home. Very few of them can take independent decisions with regards to managing the economy of the households, education of the children, marriage of grown up daughters, purchase of consumer durables etc. In case of women in domestic service sector, the windows are the women headed households who take all decisions. Limited number of households in which the male members recognise the contribution of their life partner in the house hold economy as the former conceive their inability of making both ends meet without the support of female earners in the household.

It has been observed in our study that barring occasional fringe benefits in terms of cakes, vegetables and a saree given to the maid-servant, the majority of housewives treat the female servant as unknown outsiders. They rarely treat them as a member of their family.

Low wages, longer working hours, denial of leaves and leisure, maltreatment of labour are some of the basic features of the labour employed in domestic households. Lack of unionization to be the cause of job insecurity.

As the National Commission (1987) has rightly remarked Women Domestic Workers are unprotected by law. They are in the lowest rung of the ladder in the urban economy. There is a need for making a detailed survey of such workers and necessary laws must be enacted to provide protection to such unprotected urban women workers. In addition to legal protection a change of attitude of men as well as women towards the women domestic workers is also a crucial factor.

REFERENCES

1. Tripathy, S.N.(Dr)., *Unorganised Women Labour in India* (1996) Discovery Publishing House p. 107.
2. *Ibid* p. 107-108
3. *Ibid* p. 108
4. *Ibid* p. 112
5. Tripathy, S.N.(Dr) and Das, C.R., *Migrant Labour in India* (1997) Discovery Publishing House, New Delhi.
6. Samal, K.C., *Urban Informal Sector* (1990) Manak Publishers Pvt. Ltd., p. 87.
7. Harbison, Frederick., *"Human Resources the Wealth of Nations"*, (1972) Oxford University Press, p. 76
8. Report of the National Commission, 1987, Government of India Publication Division p. 7

Chapter—5

Concluding Observations and the Policy Implication of the Study

The chapter deals with the summary conclusion and findings of all the chapters covered in the study. In addition, this chapter also delineates some policy suggestions. Though nearly half of the world's population constitutes women, yet they are unprotected, exploited and discriminated. A publication reveals the fact then women and girls are half the world's population, do two thirds of the world's work hours, receive a tenth of the world's income and own less than a hundredth on the world's property. Two out of three of the world's illiterate were women.

The status or women labourers in India is obvious from the fact that 90 per cent of them one engaged in the informal sector. Indian women do play a vital role in the Indian economy, particularly in the precarious household economics of the more than 60 million families below the poverty line. The poorer the family, the more it depends for survival on the earnings of woman. While women constitute one-third of the total labour force in India and half of the agricultural labour force, their productivity is severely constrained.

The informal or unorganised sector plays an important role in most developing economies. This is equally true for India where almost 90% of India's labour is engaged in unorganized activities and nearby one third of the country's output is estimated to originate in the informal sector. While there has been a great deal of discussion almost the precise meaning of the term informal sector, with varying interpretations, usually informal activities one characterized by their mode of organization. Moreover, these activities one usually unregulated and are inadequately represented in standard accounts of national income. In the platform of action at the U.N. women's conference in Beijing in 1995 the following was mentioned:

"Although many women have advanced in economic structure, for the majority of women, particularly those who face additional barriers. Continuing obstacles have widened their ability to achieve economic autonomy and to ensure sustainable livelihood for themselves and their dependants. Women one active in a variety of economic areas, which they often combine, varying from wage labour and subsistence forming and fishing to the informal sector. However, legal and customary barriers to ownership of, or access to, led natural resources, capital credit, technology and other means of production, as well as wage differentials, contribute to impending the economic progress of women". Women contribute to development not only through remunerated work but also through great deal of unremunerated work. On the one hand, women participate in the production of goods and services for the market and household consumption in agricultural, food production or family enterprises. On the other hand, women still also perform the great majority of unremunerated domestic work and community work, such as carrying for active to providing voluntary assistance to vulnerable and disadvantaged individual and groups. This work is often not measured in quantitative terms and is not valued in national accounts. Women's contribution to development is seriously under-estimated, and thus its social recognition is limited inadequate and poverty in the native place, are found to be the main cause of migration, supporting the `push' hypothesis of migration.

The informal women labourers one employed in handloom weaving, handicrafts, garments, food processing, construction, domestic work etc.

The important factor for women's work being limited to the informal sector is that they take opportunity to acquire skills which facilitate occupational shifts. This is depending upon the social relations between men and women and structure of economy. The analysis made in the foregoing chapters highlighting the features and problems of informal women labour brought to light that there have been disturbing tendencies regarding employment of women. The findings are as follows:

- The unemployment rate of women labourers is increasing faster;
- women labourers one being pushed out of their traditional occupations;
- causalisation of work amongst women is higher than amongst men.

As a result of which as has been observed in developing countries the rural poor failing to get absorbed in the agricultural sector and formal sector, are forced to migrate to urban centres with a view to searching employment, income and livelihood. They are mostly engaged in the retail trade like selling vegetables, pan, repairing shops, tea stalls and as casual labour in construction, shops and commercial establishments, hotels, restaurants and domestic households. All those are known as informal sector. In fact, informal sector plays a vital role in a developing country like India with its abundant supply of labour.

The vast majority of women labourers in the construction sector or domestic segments, women, labourers are prayed upon by contractors or employers who exploit their ignorance. The reasons inherent in the neglect and hardships by women labour are their lack of organization, educational backwardness low level of awareness and general invisibility.

Women who work in various sectors such as agriculture, collection of minor forest products, family firms and cottage enterprises, handlooms and handicrafts within the home and domestic service one particularly prone to 'invisibility'. Till recently, most census numeration's were listing these as housewives, where as they are major producers in their own right and are crucial to the survival of the family at the rural level. Most of the women who work in these sectors one completely untouched by state benefits as their services are not taken into account. Similarly, in urban areas such informal women labourers one isolated and out of the reach of educational awareness generation and organizational efforts due to the very nature of their work.

Some groups, such as maid servants can be commissioned or regulated but others, such as sub-contract women labourers who provides services or produce minor components one usually at the nearly of middlemen who exploit them substantially.

Many migrant domestic servants in cities live on pavements or in slum and serve other in houses. A women domestic labourer has to sweep, wash utensils and cloths of two to three households in a day. She has to repeat the same work in their own house and in other homes where she works. Sometimes, domestic workers are sexually assaulted by their employers. Thus, the helplessness of informal women labourers is compounded by gender role expectations and bound to monotonous repetitive, labour intensive, low paying work which is generally considered appropriate for women.

In the informal sector since none of the protective labour laws such as Maternity Benefit Act (1961), Employees State Insurance Act (1948), Factories Act (1948), Equal Remuneration Act (1976). The Shops and Establishment Act (1984),. The Plantations Act (1951), The Mines Act (1951), The Child Labour (Prohibition and Regulation) Act (1976) are applicable, women labourers are mercilessly exploited.

A close analysis of field data of the informal women labourers in the construction and domestic service sectors brought to light the following findings:

(i) The district Ganjam (undivided) in Orissa has 84 per cent of rural population whose main occupation is agriculture. The migrant informal women labour households of Berhampur (86 per cent) are employed in the informal sector;

(ii) Forty eight per cent of construction women labourers belong to small families comprising 6 to 8 members;

(iii) Fifty six per cent of women households belong to general caste whereas the SC and ST households constitute 42 per cent;

(iv) Fifty four per cent of women construction labourers are illiterate;

(v) Fifty two per cent of the women construction labourers are residing in a single room devoid of the basic limitation facilities;

(vi) The indebted households constitute 69 per cent among the construction women labour households;

(vii) While 48 per cent of the households are residing in the rented house only 32 per cent of the women construction labour households have their own houses;

(viii) Seventy six per cent of women labourers employed in domestic households are found illiterate;

(ix) A family size of 5 to 6 members is manifested among the women labourers employed in domestic households;

(x) Fifty per cent of women labour households earn an income in the range of Rs. 601 to Rs. 800 whereas only 20 per cent of such households are earning more than Rs. 800.

The gender inequalities and discrimination is manifested in male and female earnings. Operations which fetch higher wages are preserved for males whereas work of arduous nature organizing in lower wages is done by women. The same is the case in industries like bidi-making, construction work, cashew and coir. Here, women are assigned unskilled work, they are paid less even in skilled operations in construction work, men do the skilled jobs of brick laying while women mix mortar and carry head loads of earth and bricks.

In the light of the aforesaid analysis, it is pertinent to focus light on the government policy paradigms along with suggesting some useful measures.

Our perspective in the development of women has undergone a radical change in the last fifty five years. We have made essentially, from a welfare approach where the focus was on the role of women as mothers and wives, to an empowerment and rights based approach, where we acknowledge that women have rights. We have to recognise their rights, paving the way for their development. Empowerment, is a multifaced process which encompass many aspects-enhancing awareness, increasing access to resource-economic, social and political but of which an equally important component is the mobilisation and organisation of women into groups. This is because these groups form the basis for solidarity, strength and collective action.

Groups have emerged under various schemes and initiatives. These groups are known as self-help groups, Mahila Mandals, Mahila Surasthya, Sanghthans etc. which are acting not only as delivery mechanisms, but also as the agents of empowering village level situations mainstreaming all programmes across sectors, and focussing specifically on women specific interventions are to be adopted for the empowerment of women. The state interventions must ensure some visible effect in terms of reducing crude death rules, infant mortality rates, increasing life expectant and enhancing access to education and literacy.

Empowerment is linked to issues of social justice and equality. The principle of gender equality is enshrined in the Indian constitution, but we have over the years established institutional mechanisms to give focussed attention to these issues. To safeguard the rights and legal entitlement of women, National Commission for Women has been established. The National Human Rights Commission look into human rights issues involving women. The 73rd and 74th constitutional amendments providing reservation of seats for women in panchayats and municipalities are historical land marks in the process of securing gender equality. Transforming our attitudes is equally important in order to bring about change in the realm of gender equality.

Generating productive employment, eradication of poverty ensuring food and nutritional security for the vulnerable sections of society are some of the objectives of the common minimum needs programme of the government which would definitely result in the development and empowerment of women.

During the ninth plan special thrust was gives on expeditious adoption of the national policy for empowerment of women and towards raising their status. Over the decades of planned development the changed emphasis of women programmes from the purely welfare and consumption oriented approach to a more pragmatic and development oriented one, has recognised the women as productive workers and contributors to the country's economy.

Women Development Corporation set up in several states are also making concerted efforts towards improving the condition of women by upgrading their skills through training programmes and offering greater employment opportunities to them in schemes like public distribution, dairy development, food preservation, social forestry, rural marketing, etc. These activities are related to them in traditional occupations like agriculture, animal husbandry, fishery and others.

The government of India's National perspective plan for women (1988-2000) admits the fact that "While rural women have became marginally visible in the antipoverty programmes they have not been adequately recognised in agricultural development".

In the context of informal women labour which has increased by leaps and bounds with the process of urbanisation and industrialisation in recent decent decades, it is imperative to focus policy for urban planning which has relevance for influx of rural population due to rural urban migration.

Urban planning basically involves decisions regarding the organisation of space, and land use. There decisions should be based on vision of development. Mistaken decisions of planners with regard to locations, land use and unrealistic standards have caused a conflict between the formal and the informal sectors in the city area. The dominance of the formal sector over the planning process has pushed out or marginalised a whole group of people from the planned city. As a result, these informal sector employed households males and females both, making unauthorised colonies or 'unplanned settlements'.

A sympathetic understanding of the socio-economic problems of these working women who contribute substantially to the household economy is required for incorporating them in the planning frame work.

Special measures are to be taken in favour of informal sector by providing equal access to informal labour households. The following points may provide a direction for incorporating urban informal sector within urban planning frame work:

(i) To recognize the urban informal sector as an integral part of all master plans and development plans;

(ii) To make land use plan in such a way that it achieves maximum integration and complementarily of informal and formal sector . A liberal location policy needs to be adopted. For instance, while allocating a plot of land for a shopping complex enough space should be provided to accommodate and encourage the vendors, retailers and the construction labourers;

(iii) To recognise and support the urban informal sector in a manner such that its conflict with the formal sector is resolved. Provision of dumping yards for the waste-pickers, segregated traffic lanes for pedal rickshaws , working yards for the home-based producers are some examples of this supportive strategy.

Focusing our attention to the "informal sector'—mainly the construction women and `domestic service activities 'we have to suggest policy implications for ameliorating their socio-economic living standards.

In the context of construction women labourers the following suggestions have been forwarded:

(i) Equal pay for all types of unskilled work and schemes for skilled up gradation for women should be undertaken, through strong endorsement of laws;

(ii) Provisions of housing and creche facilities must be ensured to construction women labourers on all sites;

(iii) Existing laws should be amended to provide powers in inspection and prosecution and protection from victimisation of informal women labourers;

(iv) Violation of laws by the contractor should result in cancellation of licences and increase penalty;

(v) Hours of work for construction labour should be restricted to six hours, from early morning till noon. Safety norms should be evolved and enacted as law. Women labourers should be provided toilet, drinking water and other minimum facilities;

(vi) When fatal accidents occur, it should be made mandatory for the principal employer to inform authorities and deposit the compensation before the labour Commissioner;

(vii) Unless agricultural women labourers are educated, organised conceived regarding their right awakened, they cannot be emancipated form socio-economic bondage;

(viii) A legal literacy programme can enable women labourers to apply that vertical awareness to the law and legal process, discovering both the limits and possibilities of law in the in the battle for socio-economic change;

(ix) The construction women labourers being casual workers, are unable to claim subsistence allowance in times of financial crises, they borrow as an exorbitant rate of interest leading to indebtedness. Therefore there should be adequate social security safety-nets in the from of supply of credit, medical aid and other benefits along with their proper enforcement;

(x) As informal women construction labourers perform monotonous, strenuous back-breaking work in unhealthy working conditions, they should be provided with protective equipment for handling the construction materials.

Finally, such construction labourers should be organised for uplifting their living standards.

Services for informal women labourers in neglected sectors like construction, maidservants in our analysis, will have to be planned and formulated in a need-based manner with a flexible approach. The domestic informal women labourers should organise themselves to raise a crusade against exploitation and form trade unions for legitimate demands. Such informal workers needs to be provided some basic skill of performing their duties more efficiently and thus, the immense potentiality concealed within these women and their creativity are yet to blossom.

Bibliography

Books

Aripse, L., *"Women in the Informal Labour Sector: The Case of Mexico City"* in Wellesely Editorial Committee (ed) Women and National Development. The complexities of change, University of Chicago Press (1978).

Aziz, Abdul., *Urban Poor and Urban Informal Sector* Ashish Publishing House, New Delhi (1984).

Banerjee, Biswajit., *"Rural to Urban Migration and Urban Labour Market: A Case Study of Delhi"* Himalaya Publishing House, Bombay (1986).

Banerjee Nirmala: *"Women Workers in the Unorganised Sector: the Calcutta Experience"* Sangam Books, Hyerabad (1985).

Dak, T., *Women and Work in Indian Society.* Discovery Publishing House, New Delhi (1988).

Mathur, R.N., *Quality of Working Life of Women Construction Workers,* Commonwealth Publishers, New Delhi (1980).

Papola, T.S., *Urban Informal Sector in a Developing Economy,* Vikas Publishing House, New Delhi (1981).

Samal, K.C., *Urban Informal Sector,* Manak Publication, Pvt. Ltd., (1990).

Tripathy, S.N., *Bonded Labour in India,* Discovery Publishing House, New Delhi (1989).

Tripathy, S.N. and Das., Soudamini., *Informal Women Labour in India,* Discovery Publishing House, New Delhi (1991).

Tripathy, S.N. (Edited) *Unorganised Women Labour in India,* Discovery Publishing House, New Delhi (1996).

Tripathy, S.N: *Contractual Labour in Agricultural Sector,* Discovery Publishing House, New Delhi (2000).

JOURNALS

Arunachalam, Jaya., *Women in Informal Sector: New for Policy Options,* Social Welfare, August-Sept., 1997.

Bhatt, Ela R., *The Unprotected Labour,* The Indian Journal of Labour Economics, Vol 37, 1994.

Kulshrestha, A.C. and Singh, Gulab., *"Gross Domestic Product and Employment in Informal Sector of the Indian Economy"* The Indian Journal of Labour Economics, Vol. 42, No. 2, 1999.

Meher, Rajkishore., *'The Migrant Female Bread Winners: Women in the Informal Secondary Sector of Rourkela, Orissa'* The Indian Journal of Labour Economics Vol. 37, No. 3, 1994.

Mincer, U.J. and S. Polachek., *"Family Investment in Human Capital Earnings of Women",* Journal of Political Economy, Vol. 82, No. 2, 1972.

Pathak, Puspa and Patnaik, Indu; *Lowest Rung of the Production Process: Women Home-based Piece-rate Workers in Urban India.*

The Indian Journal of Labour Economics, Vol. 37, No. 3, 1994.

P. Thippaiah., *Women Workers in Urban Unorganised Sector,* Social Welfare, May, 1989.

Unni, Jurnol and Ravi, Uma., *Informal Sector: Women in the Emerging Labour Market.* The Journal of Labour Economics, Vol. 42, No. 4, 1999.

Yadav, Ravi Prakash., *Women Workers Worldwide,* Social Welfare, August, 1999.

Yadav, Ramnath and Azad, M.P.., *Role of Women in Allied Enterprises of Rural Development,* Kurukshetra, 36(2), Nov. 1987.

Wishwakarma, R.K., *Urban Informal Sector, Concept, Public Policy Issues and Measures,* Nagarlok, Vol. XII, No. 2. April-June, 1980.

Index